Working With Parents

Dolores Curran's Guide to Successful Parent Groups

DOLORES CURRAN

AGS®

American Guidance Service
Circle Pines, Minnesota 55014-1796

AGS staff participating in the development and production of this publication:

Dorothy Chapman, Director, Instructional Materials

Bonnie Goldsmith, Acquisitions Editor

Steven Moravetz, Marketing Associate

Charles Pederson, Copy Editor

Jill Rogness, Production Coordinator

Maureen Wilson, Art Director

Project Editor

Eileen Kuehn

Design

Terry Dugan, Terry Dugan Design

©1989 Dolores Curran
All rights reserved, including translation. No part of this publication may be
reproduced or transmitted in any form or by any means without
written permission from the publisher.
Printed in the United States of America.

A 0 9 8 7 6 5 4 3 2

Library of Congress Catalog Card Number: 89-85058

ISBN 0-88671-271-8

Contents

Contents

Introduction

Several years ago a pediatrician who was leaving his practice for another medical specialty told me why he was making a career change. "I went into pediatrics because I love children," he said. "But I didn't realize that every child comes with a parent, and I can't deal with parents. They are my biggest headache." He speaks for many of us in the caring professions, whether we are teachers, social workers, child psychologists, daycare providers, religious educators, nurses, or pediatricians. We enjoy our primary careers, but our auxiliary work with parents can be frustrating.

Parents complain, intrude, advise, and subvert our efforts. In addition, they have power. It is parents who complain to superintendents and school boards. It is parents who put pressure on clergy to clean up sex education in the classroom. It is parents who switch pediatricians and psychologists when they don't like one's professional manner or diagnosis.

Many of us in professions that require working with parents lack confidence and skills to deal with parents, either as individuals or in groups. A call from parents requesting a conference can be unsettling (even though we make the same request of them). Sports booster meetings, back-to-school nights, parent-team staffings, parent conferences—parent sessions of any kind—intimidate us because we don't know what parents are going to bring up or if we will respond effectively. Our dilemma is compounded when we ourselves are parents and we recognize the dichotomy between how we feel *as* parents and how we feel *toward* parents. I recall a routine parent conference when a teacher went on and on about my son's messy desk. I sat there smiling on the outside, seething on the inside. I felt as though I were being judged a bad parent because his desk was messy. Yet I longed to hear more about his educational and social development in third grade.

Even though professionals play important roles in children's lives, parents nominally control the vast majority of a child's waking time from the beginning of the formative years through high school. We know that when parents are supportive, our effectiveness increases. If we are social workers involved with delinquent children, we know that cooperative parents are our greatest asset. If we are religious educators, teachers, social workers, recreation and sports directors, daycare providers, or health care professionals, we recognize the primacy of parent motivation and support in achieving our ultimate goals.

Part of our professional task, then, lies in helping parents understand how to use their parenting hours in ways that are most advantageous to their children.

How did we reach the point of viewing parents as adversaries rather than allies? A brief history of parent involvement might be helpful in examining the roots of our attitudes. For most of history, the child was seen as our sole focus. As professionals, we were charged with teaching, healing, or otherwise dealing with children. Few of us were trained to work with the parents of these children. We studied the psychology and development of children, but not of parents. Many of us have a void in our professional training in this crucial area of interaction with parents. I conducted a brief survey of eleven college departments offering education degrees and discovered only three that offer a course in working with parents, and those courses were elective.

Furthermore, until relatively recently, parents were persuaded to believe that the helpful parent did not interfere with our efforts and policies. "If you come to school with blood in your eye, you go home with your child in your hand," a 1951 letter to parents warned. Institutions rarely were so blunt, but many implied that if parents didn't like the way they operated, parents were at liberty to remove their children from the institution's care. This attitude set up a defensiveness in parents that remains today.

I call this the "there-are-no-bad-kids-just-bad-parents" era. We covertly, and sometimes overtly, implied that we were the real authorities, and parents were expected to be our supporters and defenders. If a child was punished in class, we applauded the parent who punished that child again at home. It was a vote of confidence in our authority. We considered unsupportive the rare parent who listened to the child's side and questioned the fairness of the punishment. If we diagnosed a problem and prescribed treatment, parents were expected to accept it without question. If we taught a moral doctrine, we assumed parents would accept it because we were trained in moral theology, not they.

In his 1977 book, *All Our Children: The American Family Under Pressure*, Ken Keniston, representing the Carnegie Council on Children staff, wrote, "Today's parents have little authority over those others with whom they share the task of raising their children. On the contrary, most parents deal with those others from a position of helplessness. Teachers, doctors, social workers, or television producers possess more status than most parents. . . . As a result, the parent today is usually a maestro trying to conduct an orchestra of players who have never met and who play from a multitude of different scores, each in a notation the conductor cannot read. If parents are frustrated, it is no wonder: for although they have the responsibility for their children's lives, they hardly ever have the voice, the authority, or the power to make others listen to them."

Ironically, the earliest recorded group in the United States to become involved in parent education was the Society for the Prevention of Cruelty to Animals. In 1873, an abused six-year-old girl in New York, who came to be known as "little Mary Ellen," aroused the outrage and consciences of citizenry and city leaders alike. Because there were no child protection laws at the time, her case was tried under the cruelty-to-animals laws. Her foster mother was found guilty and sentenced to one year in prison. But out of the publicity and poignancy of the case was born the New York Society for the Prevention of Cruelty to Children. Its primary function was the protection of children, and to this end it became known for its intervention and prevention programs, including parent education.

Eventually, the many societies for the prevention of cruelty to animals and children became federated into the American Humane Association, a division of which remains the American Association for Protecting Children. Its executive director, Larry Brown, was instrumental in my education in working with parents, and his words and techniques will be found throughout this book.

In the past, most parent education was problem-focused and professionally instigated. If the professional had a problem with a child, the parent was called in to help solve the problem. Little preventive education was offered, and when it was, it centered on how parents could help the professional do a better job in his or her milieu, rather than on how the professional could help the parents do a better job at home. A recent article on how teachers can help parents be better parents stated, "We can teach parents how to get their children to school on time." That's probably a helpful goal, but why not broaden it to helping parents get their children to bed, to lunch, and to life on time? When we teach parents techniques that they can use at home, they assume we care about them as much as we care about our own tasks and environment.

The attitude that parents serve as adjuncts to children has changed, but old fears and behaviors linger. While we may intellectually accept that parents are our allies, we often react emotionally when they become involved in our work. We don't know the degree to which parents should become involved. We don't understand their intrusive and angry behaviors or, conversely, their apathy.

Much has been written and taught on the education and care of children. More recently, we have seen an emphasis in research on the methodology of adult learning. We know that we can't teach adults in the same way we teach children. But even the methods of adult education need refining and expanding when it comes to working with parents, because we aren't dealing with a subject like computers or Scripture. We are dealing with a living limb of the parents, their children. This field requires new methodology, which I will attempt to present in this book.

As an English teacher turned religious educator turned parent educator, I have worked with parents on many levels. Much of what is contained in this book comes from years of teaching courses in family communication, parenting styles, healthy family interaction, family stress, parent-teen relationships, and the like. Whereas many years ago I viewed parents as a troublesome part of my otherwise enjoyable work, today I find them a most pleasurable group with which to work.

More recently, my work has been with staffs and professionals who want to help develop better resources and skills for working with parents—people like you, the readers. I have found great interest among social workers, church staffs, military family support professionals, health care providers, and teachers who want to learn more about parents—what they need, fear, and feel—and how they can be helped in their task of rearing healthy children.

I've discovered that new parent educators share some common anxieties: What if parents won't talk? Am I qualified to teach parenting? Am I a sufficiently good parent myself? What if I can't answer parents' questions? How do I gain parents' trust and deal with confidentiality? What value system do I teach? How do I deal with disruptive or angry parents?

Much of the material in this book applies to good adult education, as well as parent education. I have chosen to focus on working with parents rather than with adults in general because so many of our caregiving professionals consider parents an auxiliary part of their population, and because few of us have had training in working effectively with them. I also have chosen to write for a wider readership than professional parent educators, because much prevention-based parent education today is offered by schools, churches, hospitals, mental health centers, and other institutions that use their own staffs as teachers and facilitators.

I hope the information offered in this book will allay fears of new parent educators. The fears are real, but so are the answers. The information contained here comes from people who have been in the field a long time and who have found parent education to be rewarding and fulfilling. I have learned much from you, the professionals who are caregivers in the best sense of the word. Perhaps sharing what I have learned about working with parents will help alleviate some of your fears and frustrations and make your work a little easier, the families you work with a little healthier. If so, I will have accomplished what I set out to do.

Chapter *1*

Working with Parents: Rewards and Frustrations

Whenever we gather as professionals who work with parents, we have a tendency to focus on frustrations rather than rewards, so I deliberately begin by examining the plus factors. It forces us to look at what we like about parents, to admit that parents are people like us (and indeed they are, since most of us are parents), and to grant them the value they deserve.

Thus, when I facilitate a workshop on working with parents, I usually set the tone for the session by writing on a flip chart the question, "What do you like about working with parents?" There's usually a prolonged and often uncomfortable silence, and then someone ventures, "Well, they're eager to hear about better ways of dealing with kids." Another adds, "They like to know they aren't alone in their problems." Once the idea takes hold that working with parents can be enjoyable, responses pour forth. To many professionals, this is a new experience.

Rewards

The rewards of working with parents can be grouped into a number of familiar responses:

1. Parents are motivated. "You don't have to sell parents on the idea that what you're offering is worth listening to," an early childhood educator said. "They live with their kids, and they're eager to hear any tips that make parenting easier." When we teach an academic subject, we often begin by attempting to convince our students that the material they are about to learn is relevant to their lives. When I taught English, I spent a good portion of my time answering the question, "Why do we have to learn this?" Not so with parents. They know why they are there and why discussing children's behavior, development, and skills is worthwhile. They are receptive to new ideas and eager to find answers to some of the frustrations they encounter daily in their family lives.

2. Parents are humble. "Parents don't know all the answers," a social worker said. "They can admit to ignorance when it comes to parenting. All I have to do is say, 'Has anyone had a child who wouldn't eat?' and hands go up all over the place." In other groups we find people who view themselves as authorities, but even the Ph.D. in astrophysics may have a child who folds his arms, looks his parent straight in the eye, and says, "No!" This kind of behavior reinforces humility in parents. They readily admit they need help, regardless of their power in the world outside the home.

3. Parents can laugh at themselves. What a gift being able to laugh at oneself is. Humor is essential when it comes to talking about frustrations in relationships. It gives us a sense of perspective. It distances us from ourselves and our roles.

I recall the mother who told about her son's incessant criticism of her driving. One day when he was sitting in the far back of the family station wagon, he shouted, "You went through a red light."

"It was yellow," she replied.

"Well, it was red when I went through it," he said.

Her story broke up the class of parents. We didn't have to discuss kids' exasperating expectations of parental perfection. The story told it all. And it opened the floodgates for other stories parents had to tell on themselves.

4. Parents are willing to try something new. If parents are struggling with a problem at home, and someone tells how he or she dealt with a similar experience, parents listen. Often they report back with pleasure that they tried a technique and it worked. Since most of us tend to parent in the manner in which we were parented, our bank account of skills may be slim. When we hear others tell of going through the same experience with better results, we're encouraged to try new techniques.

5. Parents never give up trying. A school nurse said, "What I like best about working with parents is that in spite of overwhelming problems, they continue to hope. I've worked with parents who have lost their jobs, live in horrible conditions, and have a kid on drugs. But they keep trying to be good parents. Sometimes I am humbled by them." I've noticed that some parents don't give up on children even though their child may be thirty years old. This optimism is a definite plus in working with parents.

6. Parents are grateful and affirming. All of us need affirmation in our work, and parents frequently supply it to our otherwise nonaffirming professions. In the recent past, for various reasons, teachers, social workers, religious personnel, and others in the caregiving professions have frequently been criticized by the media for failing to produce expected results. Where once we were granted a degree of prestige and professionalism, we are now often discouraged by hearing that we are part of the problem. Many professionals have left education, the clergy, and social work because we get weary of butting our heads against the walls of popular criticism and bureaucracy.

When we work directly with parents and are able to help them, we find they supply the affirmation we need. "'You really helped me through a tough time with my kids,' is all I need to hear to keep going," one parent educator reported. Another said, "I think there's a bit of the messiah complex in all of us, and when parents are grateful, I feel like it's all worth it."

Frustrations

After we have discussed the positives of working with parents, it's easier and less discouraging to approach the frustrations. It's the frustrations that we must battle in our daily work, so let's examine the most familiar ones:

1. Parents don't show up—and those who do, need help least. Is there anyone among us who hasn't spent hours of effort on setting up a parent meeting only to see five attend? We feel rejected and often remark to ourselves and others, "Parents say they want help, but they don't care enough to give up bowling or television to come to a conference or meeting." Or the ones who do appear don't really need what we offer, because they are the ones who are already doing a good job of parenting. We find ourselves talking to those with the least need, instead of to those who have the most to learn. The irony of the situation can paralyze us, and we end up talking together about the needs of parents who aren't there.

A 1984 Gallup Poll asking teachers to name their biggest problems found that 31 percent cited parents' lack of interest in improving their parenting skills. The cost of parent apathy is enormous to us as professionals. We begin to doubt ourselves and question our efforts. We stop trying to prevent problems and instead find ourselves dealing with more crises. Yet a small, nagging voice within us says, "Parents need help earlier, before there's abuse, depression, or divorce. What can I do to help before they reach the problem stage?" Professionals who work with dysfunctional families are the greatest supporters of preventive education. But when we offer preventive care, it often is rejected. We can take only so much rejection before we give up trying. I see this cycle in social workers, particularly. They choose their career because they like people and have something to offer. But the bulk of their time is spent on family problems that could have been prevented if the right support systems had been available when needed.

The issue of absent fathers is part of this frustration. Although we are finding more fathers attending parent education workshops and classes than in the past, our groups are still heavily weighted with mothers. One way of attracting fathers might be to hold a fathers-only session: "Being the Dad I Always Wanted," or "Fathering Daughters Today." Another way might be to emphasize in our publicity the value of fathers in the parenting process. For example, we might comment on how lucky the children are whose fathers take the time to learn more about being good parents. A third recourse is to have a couple or an unrelated man and woman as cofacilitators. Men seem more willing to attend if a man is codirecting the discussion. (I know this fact is aggravating to many, but nevertheless it is true.)

A good technique when there are two facilitators is to separate the men and women during part of the session, then reconvene and share insights. My husband and I cofacilitated a workshop recently on "Rewards and Strains in the Two-Career Marriage." (For a handout we used, see Appendix A.) After our initial presentation, we separated couples and asked them to respond to the question, "If I could change one thing about my spouse that would reduce our family stress, it would be . . ." We filled flip charts with responses, reconvened as couples, and shared the information. We had adopted a confidentiality rule that we could not identify who said what. Naturally, each spouse tried to discover which response was offered by her or his partner, but by the time we reached the fourth response, couples were chuckling because they had identified all of them as their spouse's responses. This frequently happens because stress responses are so universal. There is comfort in knowing others share the same problems and feelings.

Besides the absent-father frustration, it is sometimes difficult to attract parents to heterogeneous groups; some feel comfortable only in culturally or economically homogeneous groups and may be suspicious of mixed groups. Parents from rural areas or small communities may be apprehensive about confidentiality. To offset these fears, I often ask meeting and class planners to invite respected parents in the community to attend. Their visibility assures others that it is safe to participate.

When we work with parents who have low self-esteem and lack confidence in themselves, it is vital to begin by stressing their skills and strengths. For example: "Let's talk about what you did right last week." I once observed an exceptionally positive activity for mothers in Denver who receive Aid for Families with Dependent Children (AFDC). The mothers and their children were picked up by a van, and activities were conducted for the children while the mothers attended a cooking class. While they were preparing the food, the parent educator led the mothers into conversation relating to their children. Much good parent education took place in these weekly sessions, which were supposedly designed to teach cooking on a low budget. I know a social worker who holds a "Talking About Kids" coffee hour discussion in a room near the AFDC office on welfare-check days. She offers child care and holds an informal conversation with parents, often beginning with, "Okay, what child drove you crazy last week?"

2. Parents want one answer that always works. "It drives me crazy when a mother comes back to me and says, 'You told me to do this and I did, and it didn't work,'" a parent educator once told me. "I want to scream, but instead I try to pacify her. What's wrong with me?" He was feeding into the parent's idea that there is a single solution to a given problem. As a professional, he realized there isn't one simple answer, but his need to be an authority submerged his need to give the parent options. Our task is to enable or empower parents by giving them skills and confidence so they will not need to "go to the authority" for all answers. Parents need to feel a sense of control rather than helplessness. And they need to understand that experiencing failure is part of learning.

As we get into the empowerment process in upcoming chapters, we will see the wisdom in giving parents multiple options, as opposed to one suggestion. I'm a firm believer in telling parents at the beginning: "This may not work for you, but . . ." I also believe in giving parents a variety of responses so they will realize that their effectiveness lies in trying several alternatives, not in seeking one magic answer that will solve their specific problem.

I am reminded of the father who was having problems with his sixteen-year-old daughter. "She's running wild," he said. "She doesn't listen to me when I tell her what can happen to her. I've grounded her for months, but it doesn't help. What can I do to make her realize she's ruining her life?" My heart went out to him. He really cared about his daughter, but his sole solution to the issue was grounding her and keeping her from the activities and friends she most desired and needed. I'm happy to report that once he became aware of alternative methods of dealing with her normal adolescent behavior—mutually negotiating limits and consequences, allowing friends of dubious propriety within the home setting only, and granting her the privilege of venting her frustrations to him without fear of reprisal—life with her improved. His status as a single parent of a daughter baffled him. A former military officer, he reached for authority and regulations when she needed space and understanding. Once they were able to hear each other's expectations and needs, they were better able to reconcile differences. But it took time and patience, and parents who seek simple answers seldom have either.

I find that it's effective in working with parents to let them know immediately that there are a variety of responses to a given situation. What works for one parent or with one child may not work for another. This gets us off the hook of authority and puts parents into their rightful role of examining multiple responses, choosing those most likely to meet their needs and parenting styles.

3. Parents view professionals as rivals rather than allies. As I mentioned in the Introduction, some parents have good reason to distrust institutions and the people who represent them. Much of the past institutional behavior toward parents has changed, and not all parents look upon us with distrust. Still, when we perceive a problem or a negative behavior in a child and call the parent, and the parent denies the problem or rejects our suggestions, we often feel like adversaries rather than cooperators.

"Why is it that whenever I ask for a parent conference, parents come in with a chip on their shoulders before they even know what I'm going to say?" a teacher asked wearily. I suggest that this is probably because parents are usually called in about problems. If they don't know the reason for the conference, they suspect the worst. Fear generates defensiveness, and parents can build up a strong defensive armor between the time of the call and the conference. We can allay their fears by giving them some idea of the nature of the conference when we call.

Regrettably, some parents perceive all professionals as adversaries. Dealing with such parents will be discussed in later chapters. For now, let's label parental distrust a frustration.

4. Parents want to transfer responsibility to the professional. This troubling tendency shows up in all professions. A pastor told me of a mother who shared with him a long story about her errant son and then asked baldly, "What are you going to do about him?" Few parents are so blunt, but many hold religious leaders responsible for their children's faith and moral lives, teachers for their children's behavior and homework, and pediatricians for their children's health and eating habits. An orthodontist told me that most of the parents of the children he puts into braces expect him to monitor and enforce eating and headgear rules. "I turn the responsibility right back to them," he said. "But I lose a few when I do."

A more common situation is the "Yes, but . . ." parent who rejects all advice with, "Yes, but that wouldn't work for me because . . ." By rejecting active participation, parents are attempting to hand over responsibility to us. We must learn ways of gently but firmly returning it to its proper owners, the parents.

5. Parents are too busy to learn parenting. "Parents tell us they want parenting classes or family nights, but when we start planning, they say, 'Don't make it on Monday because that's soccer night, or Tuesday because we bowl, or Wednesday because . . .' There doesn't seem to be any good time for parents, ever," a daycare teacher said. She voiced a common complaint. In spite of what people say they need and want, they are often unwilling to give up other activities to make room for parenting help.

In researching my book *Stress and the Healthy Family*, I found that many families have overscheduled calendars. When I work with other professionals who constantly fight the overscheduled-family dilemma, I point out that when parents ask *us* to find time in *their* schedules we must not succumb to the temptation to overaccommodate. For example, I suggest to religious educators that when parents want their adolescent to be confirmed but reject parent sessions because of other activities, the educator smile empathetically and say, "Yes, I can see you have no time for this. When you do, there will be sessions here. We do this every year, and if you can find time before your daughter leaves for college, we will welcome you and her." What we are really saying is, "When confirmation is as important as marching band or gymnastics, come to us and we'll help." This returns the problem to the rightful owners, the parents.

We put our values where we put our time, but we aren't always honest with ourselves. When parents say parenting classes or their children's spiritual life are important, but relegate them to the bottom of their list of activities, they're clearly stating their priorities.

6. Parents sabotage our efforts. Sometimes we feel as if parents deliberately undermine our efforts to help their children. When we are trying hard to get unmotivated students to attend school, we find parents writing excuses for unexcused absences. Or excusing unacceptable behavior by shrugging and saying, "Kids will be kids." Or encouraging diabetic kids to ignore their diet. Or shouting at coaches who are trying to teach decent sportsmanship. Parent obstruction is costly to us because we feel devalued. We are baffled at their lack of cooperation when we're attempting to assist their children. Why should we have to serve as children's advocates when we are dealing with the people who love them the most?

7. Parents spend more time criticizing than supporting the institution. I don't agree with the validity of this complaint, but I understand why professionals name it as a frustration. We tend to hear more readily from parents with complaints than from parents with compliments. Part of this is human nature. As a weekly columnist, I tend to get letters from readers who disagree with a column rather than from those who like it. But when I go out to lecture at conventions, I meet hundreds of readers who say, "I like your column," or "I always read your column first." If I judged reader reaction on letters alone, I would believe that most of my readers were critical and even hostile.

I believe we experience the same phenomenon in parent education. If we're trying to achieve a goal and we get three or four complaints from parents, we assume the majority of parents feel negative, which may be completely erroneous. One school administrator remarked wryly on his superintendent's tendency to judge parent opinion on the basis of the number of angry phone calls he receives on a given issue. "The first is a crank call," the administrator said. "The second is a trend. And the third is a mandate. So all we need are three calls to shake up our policy."

These are the major frustrations that I hear over and over again from professionals. There are others, less often voiced, that will be mentioned in subsequent chapters. There are also many positives, say the social workers, teachers, pediatricians, religious educators, and others who work with parents. But this under-scores the importance of beginning with positives, not frustrations. I am reminded of a workshop participant who told me, "If you had started with the frustrations, I would have become so depressed I would have left. But after we talked about what we like about parents, I thought, 'Yes, we have a lot going for us.'"

Chapter *2*

Reexamining Traditional Assumptions

Many of the frustrations voiced in the last chapter spring from questionable assumptions we have inherited. If we are going to be effective in recruiting and working with parents, we need to question and perhaps discard these assumptions. At the very least we should be aware of them so that when the tendency to accept them creeps into our day, we can say, "Wait a minute. Is this assumption valid, or am I accepting it on hearsay?"

Like a myth, an assumption has enough credibility to make it believable, but not enough to make it truth. It is hazardous to assume general wisdom without questioning it in a given situation. For example, as a society we sometimes make the assumption that dual-parent families are healthier than single-parent families; that, generally speaking, children are better off with two parents than one.

But if we operate on that premise without examining it in a given situation, we are assuming that all two-parent families are healthier than any single-parent family. And that is simply not true. There are unhealthy two-parent families and healthy single-parent families. A divorce doesn't necessarily make an unhealthy family.

Let's say our task is to present a workshop about single parenting. The assumptions we hold will directly influence our success or failure. If we assume that most of the attending parents are living in unhealthy families, our words and methods will reflect our bias and we are apt to generate resentment among participants. They may feel prejudged and inadequate as parents before they are even heard. To offset this, I often begin a session with single parents with the question, "What is a strength you have as a single-parent family?" Answers come readily: "We communicate better." "We don't fight very much, and when we do, we make up faster." "We share more feelings." "We share more responsibility."

Soon the group is nodding in unison, and we have begun to build a support group based on strengths. The problems will come later, but by merely asking about strengths, the facilitator has built trust with parents. They realize that the facilitator recognizes that single-parent families can be healthy.

Examining our assumptions is a vital step in achieving effective parent education. Let's examine some common assumptions; first we will review the traditional assumption and then consider a revised version.

Traditional assumption: *"Parents don't care."* How often this statement is uttered in exasperation after an unpleasant parent confrontation or a meager meeting turnout! Repeated often enough, it can make us believe parents really don't care about their parenting or their children. When we run into eager parents, we may remark with surprise, "They really care about their kids." If we operate on the assumption that parents usually don't care, our methodology is bound to be flawed, because we will spend too much time trying to convince parents that good parenting is important, and not enough on how to achieve it.

"I get so tired of going to meetings and hearing about how important parenting is," one woman said. "We wouldn't be there if we didn't think it was important. Why do we have to spend time hearing complaints about parents who aren't there?" She has a point. When we begin a session with, "I'm sorry there aren't more parents here, but . . ." we imply disappointment with parents from the outset. It's only natural that attending parents are going to assume some guilt for their peers, but it's counterproductive to begin with guilt.

When, after intensive publicity and recruiting efforts, I face a small group, I swallow my pride and say at the beginning, "Some of you may feel disappointed and embarrassed by the small size of our group, but we can do things in small groups that we can't do in larger groups, so we have an advantage." This approach alludes to the size of the turnout without intensifying guilt. It also takes the sponsors, if there are any, off the hook of embarrassment.

Revised assumption: "Most parents want to be better parents." Most parents do care about their children and do want help in being better parents. They may not want to attend our meeting or come in for a conference, but that doesn't mean they don't care. It may mean that they have other activities, that they are fearful, or that they have been disappointed in past offerings. They may worry that their attendance implies their failure in parenting or that they will be expected to expose family problems that they have kept well concealed, especially if the community or the congregation is small. Rather than assuming they don't care, I suggest holding a telephone conference with the parents or writing them a letter. If these communications are empathetic in tone, the parents will sometimes respond to a second invitation to a face-to-face conference.

Traditional assumption: "We know the child better than the parents." Because we are professionals trained in child development and experienced in working with many children, we tend to know more about children in general than parents do. But we must remember that parents know more about their own children than we do. When we tell parents what their child is like, they often react with astonishment and resentment. In my early high school teaching experience, I remember saying to parents, "She's such a pleasant girl—always happy," and seeing their expression of disbelief. Some even remarked, "Are we talking about the same girl?" Obviously, some students weren't always pleasant at home, even if they were during the hour a day that I was with them.

More destructive is our tendency to *begin* a session or personal conference by telling parents what their children are like. "Bobby shows signs of low self-esteem. He is basically shy and insecure." This shy and insecure Bobby may have just pummelled his younger brother and stubbornly refused to admit to it.

Revised assumption: "Most parents know their own children better than anyone else does." When we operate on this assumption, we are more likely to listen to parents, and they will respond far more receptively to what we have to share. "Tell me about Bobby," we can say. "What's he like at home?" This grants parents an authority we don't have. Or, if we are in a group session, instead of beginning with, "Here's what normal six-year-olds are like," we can begin by asking, "What are some behaviors and feelings of your six-year-old?" The list will be the same, but we are clearly indicating to parents that they are the resource people and that we respect their expertise with their own children.

Often a particular child doesn't fit the profile of the "normal" child. Some two-year-olds and some fourteen-year-olds are docile. Some girls are more rambunctious than their brothers. By listening initially to parents tell what their children are like, we can help them more than by assuming we know more about their children than they do.

Traditional assumption: *"We have more answers than parents do."* Readers are going to hear me say this throughout the book: there are more solutions within any given group than within a single facilitator. We may have book and classroom knowledge of children, but parents have the live experience. They know what works for them and what doesn't, and they are usually happy to share their failures and successes with the group.

Revised assumption: *"Parents as a group have more solutions than we do."* In upcoming chapters, I'll be talking about a parent education process that is effective with groups of parents. Part of the process consists of turning a problem over to the group. Let's say a parent asks, "My four-year-old tattles all the time, and it's driving me crazy. How can I get him to stop?" Because we have knowledge and like to feel profound, we're tempted to give a short lecture on why kids of this age tattle. Instead, we would be far more effective in building a supportive group if we asked, "Has anyone else here had that problem?" Hands go up. Parents nod. "Good. Let's ask first whether it's normal or abnormal for a four-year-old to tattle." Yes, they nod. Normal.

"Okay. If it's normal, why would a child tattle?"

"For attention." "To get a sibling in trouble." "To get even." "To get praise from us for being good." "Because they're bored."

"Good answers," we respond, "and they're all valid at different times and with different children. Now let's talk about what didn't work for us with a tattler. Remember, we learn by failing, and if we can share our failures, it might prevent someone else in the group from repeating them."

"Well, punishing my tattler just made it worse." "I would listen every time and check out every situation. It just made her tattle more." "I told him I didn't want to hear any more tattles, so he didn't tell me when his sister was playing in the car and released the brake."

The group listens to the failures and then we ask, "Okay, what worked?"

"We set up two kinds of tattles—silly and real. When they came to us with a tattle, we'd smile and say, 'That's a silly, isn't it?' or

'That's a real tattle. Thanks for letting me know.' It worked for us." "I discovered my daughter tattles because she wants brownie points from me. So when she tattles now, instead of responding to the situation I hug her and say, 'I'm glad you don't do that.' It really cut down on her tattling and I don't have to referee meaningless situations." "We told our tattler he could have two tattles a day."

Once the solutions start coming in, other, more timid, parents will contribute. At some point, in fact, we may have to cut it off, saying, "Hey, folks, we've got a bunch of options here," and turning to the parent who posed the original question: "If one doesn't work, try another. And let us know what happens."

If the group is interested in the topic, and if I have more to offer, here's where the mini-lecture comes in. I may reach into my store of knowledge and give a four-minute discourse on the psychology behind tattling. But if the group is ready to move on and the asker seems content with solutions offered, I'll control the temptation to show off my knowledge and instead move on to another question.

Traditional assumption: *"Parents naturally understand child development because they have children."* Many parent educators do not subscribe to this assumption, but some do. Their attitude is, "They are the parents. They should know what children are like." They do know what their own children are like, but they don't know if behavior is normal or a problem, especially with the first child. If we assume that parents understand teenage separation behaviors, and we begin discussing reactions and responses without laying the developmental groundwork, we're not going to help parents understand that much adolescent behavior is predictable and normal.

This volatile topic can cause great stress and disharmony in the home, so when I work with parents, I approach it like this: "Adolescents don't like to behave the way they do, but there's a time clock inside them that ticks, 'I'm going to have to leave this nest and be on my own. Can I do it? How do I start? How do I help my parents let go of me? If I'm pleasant and docile, they'll never let me go, but if I'm troublesome, they'll be more willing to let me leave.' Adolescents don't understand and verbalize this, of course, even to themselves. They don't know why they behave so obnoxiously at times, but the hormones are bouncing and their feelings are scary. It's a little like the jitters we get before marriage.

As much as we love our intended spouse, we aren't sure we can handle marriage."

Then I'll say, "Let's put teenage behavior in another context. Remember when you were dating, and someone liked you a lot more than you liked him or her? How did you get out of the relationship?"

"By being rude or unkind," someone will reply.

"Exactly," I'll respond. "As long as you continued to be pleasant and nice to the person, he or she kept pursuing you. But eventually you were so unpleasant that the person was willing to let you go, and that's similar to adolescent separation."

When I do this, I am teaching child development, but without the psychological jargon that intimidates most parents. Our task is not so much to give parents research, but to touch their experiences and help them understand the normality or abnormality of a situation.

Revised assumption: *"Few parents know and understand child development."* The irony—no, make it outrage—is that we teach child development to everyone but parents. Teachers learn it. Social workers, pediatricians, and religious educators learn it, but except for a tiny percentage of parents, it's fair to say that parents don't understand normal developmental psychology.

Where are they expected to learn it? In high school? They're still struggling with their own parents then. Prenatal education? They're primarily interested in infant development, specifically physical and motor development. They want to know when their baby should go off the 2:00 a.m. feeding and when the normal baby begins to crawl. Remember when I said we must touch their experience? This means that parents are intensely interested in the development of their child at a given age. They aren't nearly so interested in the year ahead or just past.

When I was doing some research for this book with a group of parents, a mother handed me a note as she left. It read, "Please, in your book on working with parents, include parents of preschoolers even if it requires Volume I and then Volume II. Also, would you include a resource list in the back on how and where parents can get specific information on the development of any age child?"

Parents want to know if their seven-year-old is behaving normally at age seven. We call this a teachable moment. We can assume that most parents of seven-year-olds share similar

concerns and experiences. So why not give them the information
they need and welcome at this point?

When parents come to a back-to-school night, instead of telling
them about curriculum and grading systems, why not give them
insights into predictable behaviors and feelings of the seven-,
eleven-, or seventeen-year-old? Why not, in school, religious
education, and pediatric care, at the beginning of the school year
send home a short description of physical, emotional, and
educational development of each age level? The resources are
available. Why not devote a parent-social worker conference to
the developmental stage of each child within the family, discussing predictable behaviors and appropriate parental responses?
Such a discussion might offset tensions that result in disharmony
and even abuse, which then require corrective intervention.
Prevention is based on knowledge, correction on lack of
knowledge.

If public schools, religious schools, pediatricians, social agencies, and daycare centers all focused on educating parents to their
children's development at a given age, we would go a long way
toward achieving our goal of preventing problems rather than
having to deal with them. Most parents don't know whether a
behavior is normal or abnormal until it ends, a situation that can
be attributed to our professional omission. We understand child
development, but we reserve it for ourselves. We need to teach it
actively and positively without fomenting fear. Once parents
realize that a bothersome behavior at a specific age doesn't
necessarily mean their child will end up in the penitentiary, they
are better able to accept and effectively deal with that behavior.

A personal example here. When my eldest, Teresa, was eleven,
she began to be exacting and critical. If I said, "You're a half-hour
late," she corrected, "Twenty-six minutes." If I was relating a story
about something that happened a week earlier, she interrupted
with, "That was Tuesday, not Wednesday." And woe to me if I
accidentally called her by a sibling's name. I mistook her
preoccupation with exactness for premature adolescent disrespect and felt it had to be stopped in its tracks. Much
unnecessary unpleasantness ensued between us.

Before the birth of her next sibling three-and-a-half years later,
I happened to read the work of psychologist John McCall on the
"eleven-year-old canon lawyer," in which he described exactness
as a trait of this age and talked about the unnecessary frustration
it causes parents. He pointed out that the stage is brief (it was,

although it went into more baffling stages later), but normal. Recalling that year, I cannot appreciate enough our fifth-grade teachers who live with whole classrooms of canon lawyers who must spend most of their time saying, "It's page 110, not 109." But I do know that when my son Patrick reached eleven and followed the same pattern, I merely sighed and ignored it. I had learned a simple fact of child development that, had I understood it with Teresa, would have prevented many confrontations over disrespect. I believe the same is true with other parents. If they realize that behaviors are normal and predictable, they will deal with them less fearfully than if they are unfamiliar with the stages of child development.

One technique I use when parents ask about a problem with a child is to turn it over to the group, with the question, "Is this normal behavior for a ten-year-old?" If they agree that it is, I point out that trying to change the behavior is asking the child to behave abnormally for the age. If it's normal behavior, we can seek relief by changing either the environment or our response to the behavior. If the group agrees that the behavior is abnormal, then we discuss ways of changing the behavior.

An example: A couple in their mid-thirties with an only child, two-and-a-half years old, complained that, while they cherished a long Sunday brunch at a nice restaurant during which they read *The New York Times*, their Jeremy didn't cooperate. The mother said: "Every Sunday before we go, we say, 'Okay, Jeremy, what don't we do at the restaurant?' and he says, 'I don't screw up.' But when we get there, he pokes at our newspaper, walks around to other tables, and acts impossible. We want him to enjoy brunch with us, and we don't want to give it up because it's our favorite part of our week. What can we do?"

By the time she had finished, other parents were grinning openly. "Is this normal behavior for a two-and-a-half-year-old?" I asked.

"Yes!" they responded forcefully.

"Do you want Jeremy to behave abnormally?" I smiled at her. "No," she laughed, "but we want a normal brunch."

"Then let's look at how you can change the environment or your response to his normal behavior." I turned it over to the class. "How can they enjoy brunch and allow Jeremy to remain normal?"

"Get a baby-sitter."

Her response: "We don't want to do that because we both work, and Sunday morning is our family time together."

"Okay, how do they brunch together with a normal two-and-a-half-year-old?"

"Go to the park," one parent said. "Go to a place like McDonald's where two-and-a-half-year-old behavior is normal," said another. "Pick up food at a deli and have your leisurely morning brunch at home for a while," said a third. "Bring a young sitter along who can take Jeremy off your hands when he gets restless," another offered. "Go for brunch but read the paper at home," was a final suggestion.

After we heard a variety of solutions from the group, we talked about putting toddlers in adult environments like church and nice restaurants and expecting them to behave like adults because of the environment. The group itself concluded that when we put unlikely expectations on children, we're asking for stress. The empowerment process offered this couple permission to have a normal child—to their relief. Jeremy's behavior arose from his developmental stage, not their parenting.

I then asked the question, "Suppose Jeremy were eight years old. Is it normal for an eight-year-old to behave as Jeremy did at two-and-a-half?"

"No," the group responded.

"Then we need to deal with the behavior, not the situation. If your eight-year-old grabs at your paper and wanders around to other tables, what do you do?"

Again, a variety of responses ensued. Distinguishing between behavior and environment ended up being the most valuable content of that session, and it sprang from a parent's question. Although the question seemed a bit silly to the other parents at the time, I had several tell me later that asking the question, "Is this normal for our child's age?" was helpful in determining whether to change the behavior or the situation. (One set of parents returned a few weeks later with the insight that the reason they disliked their son's birthday party so much was that *they* were expected to behave abnormally for their age.)

I use a simple diagram in teaching the normal/abnormal concept:

Normal Behavior	*Abnormal Behavior*
Change situation.	Change behavior.
or	
Change reaction to behavior.	

If the behavior is normal at a specific age, but parents attempt to change it, they are attempting to instill abnormal behavior. The visual representation is helpful to parents who may be confused by terminology alone. (For an example of a handout on "ages and stages," see Appendix B.)

Traditional assumption: *"Parents believe what we say because we are educated authorities."* Of all the assumptions, this can be the most costly. Parents may hear what we say, but that doesn't necessarily mean they believe us. They are very good at putting on a proper face and pretending to be receptive, while remaining skeptical within.

This assumption can be particularly acute for educators who are not parents. Frequently, such educators will confide that they feel defensive in teaching parents about children because of parents' suspicion of anyone who hasn't lived with children of their own. Professionals who are not parents need not feel defensive; after all, they have objective experience. Parents have subjective experience—they know a lot more about their own children than we do. But because of our professional experience, we know more about children in general than they do.

I suggest to parent educators who do not have children of their own that, to parents who say, "Well, if you had children, you would understand . . ." they respond:

"You're right. I don't have your children, and you do know a great deal more about living with them than I do. However, after teaching (or doctoring, or whatever) for fifteen years, I figure I have interacted with close to 500 children of this age, so perhaps I can share with you some typical behaviors, problems, and responses. You tell me if your children fit this behavior. You live with your two children. I work with many. What can we learn from one another?"

Nonparents in the field of parent education must—I repeat, *must*—rid themselves of defensiveness or it will haunt their work and diminish their success. I also suggest they offset this presumed disadvantage by beginning a session or conference with, "I'm not a parent—in a blood sense, at least. I've never lived with children as an adult, so you have much to teach me. However, I have worked with 300 eight-year-olds during the past ten years, so I have some objectivity and perception of what this age is like. Perhaps we can talk about how your child interacts within his or her age group."

Parents do not have objective experience. Most don't know whether their child is more or less developed physically, emotionally, or educationally than peers. But we do, and that gives us our credibility. It's not whether we have children. But we need to internalize this confidence. If we waver when parents accuse us of inferiority because we aren't parents, it shows up in every conference and session.

Furthermore, when we are confident of our right to counsel and teach parents, it gives them confidence in us. They don't want help from an insecure source. To contrast two situations: I once had an intern, extremely talented, knowledgeable, and empathetic— but young. She felt intimidated by parents because of her youth and single status. Her approach was apologetic, and in spite of her admirable background in early childhood education and the potentially valuable guidance she could offer parents, her very bearing diminished her success. She allowed herself to question her qualifications simply because she was not a parent.

On the other hand, I worked with a nun who had little background in parent education but was a great success with parents because she felt she had something to offer. "It doesn't matter whether I've had children or not," she told parents bluntly. "I was a child. I work with children, and I know something about them that I want to share with you." Her confidence exuded competence, and parents trusted her implicitly.

There will always be parents who try to put parent educators on the defensive, even those who are parents, by saying, "Yes, but your children are young. Just wait until they're teenagers," or "But you have boys. You don't know what girls are like," or "You only have two? Wait till you have five children." We must not allow ourselves to question our competence because of such remarks. These are parental offensives and don't call for our defensiveness. When we are comfortable with our goals and qualifications, we don't let others disturb our confidence.

Someone once said, "You don't have to be a criminal to help criminals." It's a good comment to cite when our own credentials are questioned. We don't have to be parents to teach parenting. Indeed, many parents cannot teach other parents. Having children is not the primary qualification. Having knowledge, skills, and confidence in ourselves is what makes us successful parent educators.

Revised assumption: *"Parents will test everything we say against their own experience."* Although parents may be intensely interested in the information we have to share, they have a control lab at home—their children. It is only natural that they will apply our words to their children. So if we tell them that children want limits and consequences, but their children resist those limits and consequences, parents will question our expertise. I usually can tell when this happens in a group because a parent or the entire group will take on a skeptical expression that tells me they aren't fully accepting what I'm teaching. At this point, I stop and say, "Does this fit your experience or am I off the mark?"

Usually someone will say, "If they want limits, why do they fight them so much? My kids don't want limits." Another teachable moment. "Do the rest of you agree?" I ask. Nods abound. "Okay, let's look at this behavior for a minute. Is it possible to both want limits and fight them? Can anyone give an example in adult life where we do both?"

If nobody comes up with anything, I say, "Well, let's look at speed limits. Do we want speed limits?" They smile and nod, grudgingly. "Why?" I ask. "If we didn't have them, it would be a jungle out there," someone will respond.

"How many people here want speed limits?" Most hands go up. "How many people here go over the speed limit occasionally?" I ask. All hands go up.

"Why?"

"Because there's no police around." "Because I'm in a rush." "Because it's safe. There's no other traffic." "Because I daydream and find myself with a heavy foot." "Because I'm angry over something."

"All right," I say, "that same kind of behavior appears in children." Then I launch into a mini-lecture on how we test rules even though we want them, that it's natural human behavior and doesn't mean children want a home without limits. I take parents back to their high school experience and talk about teachers who had clear rules and those who allowed havoc in the classroom. "Which did you respect most?" I ask.

I share the story of the time my teenage son got a phone call, turned to me, and asked, "Mom, the guys are going to the mountains for a cookout. Can I go?"

I nodded absently. My son, however, put his hand over the receiver and whispered to me, "Say no." He was counting on me to ask more questions and to refuse permission because he sensed he shouldn't go. He trusted me to limit him, even though he asked to go. Obviously, there was something about the cookout, maybe beer, that made him suspect he shouldn't be there.

Once parents understand this natural behavior on the part of children, they are ready to go on and talk about setting limits. When they face resistance in the future, they may recall what we said and accept that resistance is natural, that it doesn't mean children don't want limits and consequences. I may even go on and talk a little about the anxiety children feel when they have too much control and parents too little.

We must stop and deal with parent skepticism at the moment it arises or whatever we say will be dismissed silently with, "She doesn't know my children."

Watch for expressions of skepticism. They are the best indicators we have. Don't hesitate to stop the session and say, "Is this in tune with your experience?" Sometimes these unplanned discussions end up being the most valuable part of parenting sessions for parents.

If we are in conference with a parent and make a suggestion, only to see it lukewarmly received, we can stop and say, "You seem reluctant. Do you think this might not work with your child?"

"No, it won't work. He'll just walk out of the room and slam the door."

"Well, let's talk about that. What do you do when he does that?"

"What can I do?"

Here is the teachable moment. The issue is not the rule, but the parent's inability to deal effectively with the child's reaction. So we focus on giving the parent possible techniques to deal with the child's reaction to rules.

Traditional assumption: *"Parents want answers more than anything else."* When we listen to parents' laments and perceive the root of the problem, we are often astonished to find that they don't want to accept our reasoning and advice. It is then that we're tempted to conclude that while parents say they want help, they really don't. They take the slightest suggestion of parental error as criticism and become defensive rather than cooperative.

Revised assumption: *"Parents want support before information."* Support is the primary reason parents attend a conference or workshop on parenting. Support implies shared experience, understanding, empathy, and help. When we present ourselves as the authority with psychology and statistics, we impair support. When we present ourselves as fellow sojourners who have experienced and empathized with the frustrations parents voice, we have them in our court. We say, "I remember when I went through that," or "I felt the same way when . . . ."

Studies of parents who have taken workshops in parenting indicate that the support they receive has higher value than the information they hear. On a personal note, because I am best known for my work on healthy families, I realize that parents from less-than-healthy families are often intimidated by attending a session on traits of a healthy family. So one of the first comments I make is, "My book *Traits of a Healthy Family* is not autobiographical. I have three children, and we have been through most of the normal problems and turmoil families face. Our kids have a parent educator for a mother and a school administrator for a father. Talk about teacher/preacher kids! Let me say up front that we have had calls from both the school and the police. Does that make you feel better?"

Group relief is visible. My admission invites support from them which, in turn, generates support for one another. As I will discuss later, this revised assumption does not imply that content is unimportant. It is important, and we need to teach it, but only after we have developed a support relationship with and among parents.

Traditional assumption: *"Parents should be mature enough to accept criticism gracefully."* Don't believe it. Few parents, ourselves included, welcome criticism of their children, even when they suspect they are in error. When a pediatrician chides a mother for failing to get medicine down her sick toddler, she may accept the chiding with apologetic grace but inwardly she's seething, thinking, "You tell me how to get it down this wriggly, resistant child. I've tried everything I know, and I've given up."

When a teacher suggests that a child is watching too much television, parents know they are being criticized, and they will rapidly become defensive and uncooperative. Our success in changing parenting habits is diminished when we're working with defensive parents. My face still burns when I recall the time, many years ago, when I bluntly told a pair of parents at conference time that their teenage son was behaving obscenely in words and gestures toward girls in the class. Instead of approaching it as a mutual problem, I said, "Your son uses obscene gestures and words with girls in class and this cannot be permitted. What makes him do this?"

My question implied parental failure, insinuating that the parents were allowing him to do this. The mother went white and the father red with rage. "That's your problem," he retorted angrily. "We're here to talk about his grades." If I were repeating the scene today, I would say, "At this age some boys think it's clever and grown-up to make sexual remarks to girls. When this happens in class it can be contagious, with each boy trying to outdo the other. Do you think you can help me in dealing with this?" This approach puts the parent in an advocacy position and softens the pain of criticism.

Revised assumption: *"Parents find criticism painful and are apt to react negatively to it."* Practicing and developing a noncritical and nonjudgmental attitude is a must in dealing effectively with parents, even with court-ordered abusive parents. This skill gets easier as time goes on, because we learn ways of phrasing sentences that don't raise parent hackles. We get rid of red-flag words and phrases like, "You ought to . . ." "Kids shouldn't . . ." "Your responsibility lies . . ." We learn to replace them with softer phrases like, "Maybe we can . . ." "Sometimes kids will . . ." "Perhaps I can help."

When parents criticize us for our methods and attitudes, we react defensively too. Often their criticism is generated by ours, and the conference degenerates into personal charges and countercharges instead of mutual solutions to the problem.

These are the most familiar traditional and revised assumptions in our relatively new field of working with parents. If we find ourselves locked into any of the traditional assumptions above, we may better understand why some of our past interaction with parents has been less effective than we desired. Rethinking our assumptions may be the key to more effective interaction with parents in the future.

Chapter *3*

First, We Listen

Let's assume that you have been handed the task of "setting up something for parents" in your church, school, or agency. What is your first response? Probably to find a speaker, pick a night and a meeting place, and publicize the offering as a two-hour session. Mentally, you visualize making coffee, arranging cookie platters, and setting up chairs.

Resist the temptation. This lecture-followed-by-questions format represents the most familiar and least effective form of parent education and is a main reason so few parents show up or return. Occasionally (very occasionally), an extremely well-known and gifted speaker will attract and entertain a large group of parents, but these speakers are few, hard to obtain, and expensive.

For three reasons the familiar lecture-question format produces disappointment in parents and planners alike. First, the speaker and planner determine parent needs, not the parents. As one who is frequently invited to be the speaker, I have memorized the phone call inviting me. It goes like this: "We're having an evening for our parents and we heard you were a good speaker. What topics do you address and suggest?" This approach turns the agenda over to the speaker, who knows little about the needs of parents in a given school or other institution. "What do you see as the needs of your parents?" I will ask. Often there's a pause and then a halting response, "Well, I'm really not sure . . ."

The first step in any parent education effort should be identifying needs, which vary vastly, and then obtaining the best speaker (if you even need one) or parenting program to address these needs. Depending on local circumstances, one community might need help with juggling finances and maintaining close family ties in spite of shift work or dual-paycheck parents. They may want help in knowing more about good, affordable child care, about how to handle jobs when children are sick, and about alleviating latchkey worries. Another might want help in learning to control calendars and prioritize activities. Still another may worry about teenage beer drinking, high-speed driving, and sexual pressures. And parents in most communities may be interested in more effective family communication.

How do you, as chief planner, identify these needs? There are several methods, depending on your time and the agency's or institution's support. Beginning with the most complex and going to the more simple, they are:

Detailed survey. This format gets down to specifics and may be sent home to all parents, although it isn't always necessary to send it home. Presenting it to parents at sign-up or registration time at clinics, recreation functions, or back-to-school nights has the advantage of catching parents at an opportune time so you can obtain the completed surveys before they get lost in the pile of junk mail we all collect. The detailed survey can be used with individual parents too; for example, in social worker-client interviews. It saves a lot of time when parents identify needs and we don't have to search for the problems.

The detailed survey usually begins with a given topic, like discipline or drugs, and attempts to isolate the parents' specific areas of concern. My survey on family stress (see Appendix C) might serve as an example. I developed it for one church and have used it in a dozen churches since, when I have been invited to present sessions on family stress. In one church, so many checked the item on Little-League-type activities that we offered a session, not on family stress in general, but on "Who Owns Our Family—We or Little League?" We drew over 200 parents because we touched the experience and frustrations of parents in that given church. We described the session as: "A look at the rewards and frustrations of children's activities, particularly as they affect the dinner hour, weekend, and family time together. Some families control these well. Let's find out how."

Another church found that television was a big problem, so we offered, "Who Controls the Knob? A Look at the Role of Television in Healthy Family Life."

Note that the survey goes beyond "yes" and "no" answers to "very important," "somewhat important," and "not at all impor-tant." If we use yes and no responses, most parents will respond

"Yes, this is a problem" to most items, so we have little way of knowing which is more troubling. When surveys are returned we can immediately discard those issues that are marked "Not at all important," even if we have no clear topic rising to the top. Too often, those of us in charge perceive issues of concern that parents don't. If we don't ask about and listen to parent needs, we guess at them, offer a program, and then feel frustrated when parents don't respond in numbers and enthusiasm. A survey helps us isolate those issues that really concern parents.

For those interested in broader survey instruments, see David Olson's *Family Inventories* and J. Daryl Furlong's *A Ministry of Listening*, both included in Resources. Furlong's book has a specific church orientation, but with a bit of editing, the instruments and evaluations would be useful in many institutions.

Simplified survey. For those who don't have the need, time, or resources to conduct a detailed survey, the following may serve:

Improving Your Children's Behavior

Following are ten topics related to parenting and disciplining children. Please mark them in order of your needs and interest (1 being most important and 10 least important):

____ Setting rules, limits, and consequences

____ Dealing with my own or my children's anger

____ Fighting among the kids

____ Hassles over chores and responsibilities

____ Sibling rivalry and jealousy

____ Disagreement between spouses on discipline

____ Being fair as a parent

____ Not carrying through on consequences

____ My fatigue and impatience

____ Television arguments and rules

A survey like this is easy to construct and tabulate. It doesn't intimidate parents because it presumes we all face these issues, and it requires only a few minutes to complete. It gives us enough information to zero in on specific behaviors. Obviously, one session with parents cannot deal effectively with all the issues listed, but the top three or four could be incorporated into a single session.

Personal interviews. If we don't want to do a written survey, we can ask parents verbally what topics they would like addressed. Usually a school, agency, or church staff agrees to ask this question of four or five families with whom they work, and then report back to the planner. It's helpful for planners to give these parents some categories and the question: Which of these interest you the most?

_____ Handling family money

_____ Getting our calendar under control

_____ Improving children's self-esteem

_____ Sharing responsibility in the home

The information gained will be more general than with written surveys, of course, but it gives planners a direction they would not otherwise have had.

Leadership consultation. Finally, if there's not enough time for any of the suggested methods, ask staff members and heads of committees what they perceive as needs. In a school system, you might ask teachers, administrators, PTO officers, heads of departments, and, perhaps, students, if they are old enough to respond. In a church, ask the ministers of education, music, and youth, as well as officers of the many organizations found in the usual membership. Sometimes these people will contact members of their groups and ask their feelings on needs. The broader our base, the closer we touch people's needs.

A second problem with the speaker-question format is that it usually consists of forty-five minutes of lecture and thirty minutes of questions. Since the questions don't come until after the lecture, we don't know people's needs and interests until we've finished presenting our material. Many a speaker is dumbfounded to discover, after presenting a brilliant lecture, that the listeners are interested in one insignificant (to the speaker) reference or, indeed, in issues not addressed at all. This experience calls to mind a speakers' joke.

Spouse: "How did your talk go, Honey?"

Speaker: "Which talk? The one I prepared? The one I gave? Or the one I gave in the car on the way home?"

The one given in the car on the way home is the one that would have addressed group interest. We may wish we could start over again in preparing our presentation because now we know what needs people want addressed. Their agenda and the one we prepare without their input are often out of sync.

A third and final problem with the speaker-question format involves the attitude of incoming participants. Many parents relate this format to high school and college classes. They expect a classroom situation, so they adopt classroom behaviors, such as boredom, daydreaming, fear of breaking into the speaker's carefully prepared lecture, clock-watching, and a hurried exit when the bell rings. Good, effective parent education cannot rely on this format. Parents want to learn, but they also want to be heard, to share wisdom and experience, and to go away feeling like adults, not students. They want their needs addressed, not general information on family life that may not resemble theirs at all. Most of all, they want support.

So, presuming that you have done your listening and isolated a specific topic, what next? Choose your facilitator carefully. Or, better yet, facilitate the session yourself, using the empowerment process described in the next chapter. If you decide to go with an outside speaker, choose one who has a reputation for listening to participants at the beginning and throughout the session, not one who reserves discussion for the question period. Say politely, "We find that our parents don't respond well to a straight lecture format. Would you be able to open your presentation to them throughout the evening and go with their needs and interests?" If the speaker is uncomfortable with this flexibility, I caution you to look elsewhere. More and more presenters are learning to step away from the lectern and establish group discussion, with good results. If you must choose between a well-known lecturer and a lesser-known professional who employs the processing approach, I say go with the latter.

When we talk about processing, the idea of obtaining a speaker becomes less important. Chances are, you or one of your staff has the skills to process if you grant yourself the competence. A lecturer is valuable for large groups and for presenting content, new ideas, and inspiration. Lecturers are highly prized in academic subject areas, but not in parent education where the subject is people and their interaction. If the speaker views parents as students and ignores interaction, parents come to believe the speaker cares more about research than about their needs and experiences.

If, instead of the lecture-question format, you think I'm going to suggest that you place parents in small groups, you're mistaken. My experience tells me that most people (and parents most of all) dislike small groups. How prevalent this attitude is I discovered after writing a whimsical column, "And Then God Said, 'Get Into Small Groups.'" Reader response was astonishing in both volume and intensity.

Why do people dislike small groups? Because so many are misused. Often they are used for little reason other than to break up the lecture format. Participants sense this. "Small groups are busy work for adults," one participant said bluntly. Other reasons for widespread dislike are that small groups can deteriorate into mindless chatter, monopolization by one talker, sharing of ignorance, or the great fear of parents—the compulsion to divulge personal experiences about one's marriage and family.

If we must use small groups with parents, then let's observe some common-sense rules:

1. Use small groups only when there is a group-acknowledged and group-accepted purpose. Sometimes the group itself will say, "We need to wrestle with this in smaller groups." That's the time to put aside our agenda and listen to theirs.

2. Avoid using small groups at the beginning of a session; you may want to break into small groups after the larger group has become bonded.

3. Acknowledge at the beginning that some people dislike small groups and give these people an alternative, even if it is only assembling as a small group to share their common dislike of small groups.

4. Use the material that the groups generate. I realize this sounds silly, but how many times have we congregated into small groups only to have our conclusions ignored because of lack of time or interest? This reaction clearly informs participants that they are in small groups for structural rather than useful purposes.

So let's discard the idea of small groups for the time being. But if the speaker-question format and the small-group format are largely ineffective in parent education, what does work? You have been handed the task of "setting up something for parents." You have ascertained through listening that your population's need is, for example, better communication in the family. What do you do with this need? If you aren't going to get a speaker, what are you going to do? Read the next chapter to discover a method that works well with parents.

Chapter *4*

An Empowerment Process That Works

The parent empowerment process assumes that the agenda and solutions come from the parents, and the professional content comes chiefly from the facilitator. It assumes that the facilitator begins by pulling the agenda out of the group, rather than stating the agenda. It means that the facilitator gives up a forty-five minute lecture in favor of six or eight five-minute lectures. It requires confidence and willingness on the part of the facilitator to step away from the lectern and notes, in favor of trusting the group's experience, interests, and needs. The process is simple and can be used with groups of up to sixty. I have used it with larger groups, but when I do, the response comes mainly from the front half of the room or auditorium.

The empowerment process requires some form of flip chart or blackboard that is visible to all. If you are anticipating a large group, this procedure is not workable. In that event, you may go to the lecture format or break your group into two or three segments. But remember, these are options.

I was once asked to consult with religious educators in a huge parish. They were experiencing tremendous resistance to parent education on the topic of children's faith development. I discovered that the educators were doing three things: requiring parents to attend three sessions, or their children could not attend church school; drawing an average attendance of 150 parents; and offering excellent lecturers, although parents rarely asked questions. The situation reminded me of the high school assembly. These parents were, in essence, "court-ordered parents," and their resentment was palpable. They listened resentfully and responded with muteness.

It was apparent to me that the most immediate problem was group size. We initiated two changes and experienced a turnaround in parent attitude. First, we held three sessions of fifty parents each. Second, we used the empowerment process instead of the lecture. Parent resistance and resentment diminished. They felt listened to rather than talked to. Of course, three sessions are more work than one, and processing takes more effort than lecturing. But if our first concern is our parents and if we feel we are not reaching them effectively, we need to examine our methods.

Before we go into the mechanics of the empowerment process, I want to mention the most fundamental goal of parent education—building a support group. Because this supersedes content, our immediate task lies in bonding the group, finding and surfacing its common denominator, and making parents feel part of the whole. The process itself serves this role, but sometimes it's worthwhile to spend some time on the "forming" stage of a group, especially if the course is five or six weeks in duration. (For more on the forming stage of groups, see Chapter 7.)

Those who have worked with groups recognize a variety of participants. Some arrive in groups, others as couples or with a friend. There always seem to be a few in any given group who enter the room timidly, take chairs in the rear, and leave quietly after the session, before the coffee. Our task as facilitators—a term I prefer to teacher or speaker—is to draw these people in and make them feel comfortable with the group. One way of doing this is to ask, after introductions and housekeeping details, "Is there anyone here who doesn't know anyone else?"

As they raise their hands, we can ask them to tell us their names and the ages of their children. Then I say, "Now everyone here knows who you are, and I suspect by the time you leave, you'll have more new friends than you may ever care to have." The more outgoing participants in the group will pick up the cue and drift toward loners during break and coffee time. By acknowledging loners publicly, we are saying, "You are one of us and we want to know you." This is often enough to draw them into the group. Going alone to a group where others seem to know each other requires an act of courage. People who leave a group after two hours without meeting and interacting with anyone aren't likely to return.

If the group is fewer than thirty, another effective technique is to invite all the parents to identify themselves and give the names and ages of their children. People "click" into other parents with children of similar ages. In bonding the group, it is vital for the facilitator to get off the pedestal early. I do this by introducing myself, giving a little background (not degrees, which tend to intimidate people, but a short history of how I happened to get into parent education), and using a technique that I borrowed from Larry Brown, executive director of the American Humane Association.

I ask parents to jot on a slip of paper the names and ages of their children. I do this on a flip chart first, using my own children's names and ages, like this:

Teresa 27

Patrick 24

Dan 20
———

Total 71

I add the years aloud and say, "I have seventy-one years of parenting experience. Now you add yours and tell me if there's anyone here who beats me." Someone may offer, "I have seventy-two," another, "eighty-five," and so on. I acknowledge the parent with the most years by saying, "We have now identified our resident expert." This parent's reaction usually generates laughter that is valuable in bonding.

Next I say, "How many have fifteen years? Twenty? Twenty-five?" and so on. Then comes the kicker. I look around the room and say, "Judging from what we've heard, I estimate we have over 600 years of shared parenting experience in this room. There's little I am going to say that someone here hasn't experienced in family life. So let's share our wisdom and our failures. I expect to learn a lot from you." A good facilitator views himself or herself as a facilitator of human growth and development, rather than as the keeper of the content. To repeat what I mentioned earlier, this is also a good time to say, "I may be a social worker or a pastor or a pediatrician, but I want you to know I have normal children with normal problems. Believe me, I am not a candidate for either Mother or Father of the Year. I've made a lot of mistakes in parenting, and I expect I'll make more. I'll share mine, if you'll share yours."

This kind of admission enhances our credibility with parents rather than damages it, as some facilitators fear. We need to avoid as much as possible the idea that we represent the Perfect Parent.

I follow these comments with, "I'd like to suggest some simple rules:

1. We can disagree and still like and respect one another.

2. Nobody has to talk.

3. Everyone who wants to talk gets to talk once before anyone gets to talk twice.

4. Nobody has to defend his or her right to an opinion.

5. We can share with friends outside our group what was said, but we agree not to identify who said what.

6. I won't be afraid to disagree or say that I don't know, if you won't be afraid to do the same.

Do you accept these rules?"

I have never had a group do anything but nod in agreement. Often there's a collective sigh of relief in the group after hearing the rules.

As I have said, out of the empowerment process emerges both the agenda and the solutions—from the group rather than from the speaker and planners. Following is a sketch of a typical process session.

Let's assume the title of the workshop is "Parents and Teens: Learning to Enjoy Each Other." Using a flip chart or blackboard, I begin by asking the group, "What do you like most about having a teenager around?" As they offer responses, I write them on the flip chart. The following are likely to appear:

> Humor
> Enthusiasm
> Energy
> Idealism
> Challenge
> Friends
> Conversation

When the group becomes quiet, I may say, "There are a couple I would like to add," and then write:

> Unpredictability
> Independence

(Because I have an agenda of my own, it's often necessary to add issues I plan to discuss that may not emerge from the group.)

I draw a line down the middle of the board or go to a second flip chart and ask, "Okay, now, what frustrates you about living with teenagers?"

Someone will inevitably name one of the characteristics listed as a positive or say, "All of the above." Laughter generally follows. This is an important moment because the group itself draws the conclusion that the positives have a flip or negative side. If we want the positives, we have to live with the frustrations—a lesson parents know intuitively but don't always verbalize. I then go through the positives and negatives of each trait with the group, asking, for example, "What do you like and dislike about teenage humor?" When we finish, the chart may look like this:

	Like	*Dislike*
Humor	Fun to have around. Gives me a lift.	Funny at wrong time. Destructive humor.
Enthusiasm	Gives zest to life.	All that energy drives me crazy at times.
Idealism	Gives me hope.	Unrealistic. Doesn't know what real world is like.
Challenge	Makes me rethink some of my opinions.	Argues with anything I say.

We continue to discuss the frustrating side of teen behaviors and perhaps add others from the group:

Laziness
Irresponsibility
Moodiness
Refusal to listen

When we have completed these two steps, we have bonded the group by surfacing their feelings and experiences, and we've shown them respect by listening to them before talking to them.

From here on, our work is easy. I examine the two lists and say, "Obviously we can't cover everything here, but many are related. Let's combine a few, such as challenge, idealism, and independence. Let's talk about these, and why they are so common in the adolescent years."

Here is where I go into professional content on the developmental process of adolescents, a mini-lecture on the need for an identity separate from the family and the various ways teens emotionally and physically begin to separate from parents. For example: by arguing, by refusing to go along on family outings, by stating Democratic Party preference when the family has always been Republican.

As I discuss this behavior, I invite examples from the group and ask for questions. Some parent is likely to ask, "But what do you do if you want to go on a family vacation and your son doesn't want to go? He can sabotage your vacation if you force him to go, but you can't leave him home alone." This is when we turn to the group for solutions. "Have any of you experienced this? What worked? What didn't work?"

Responses lead the facilitator into another mini-lecture on negotiating and collaborating with adolescents, a skill most parents desire, but few possess.

I may role play with the parent at this point, asking her to take on the role of her adolescent, and I, the parent. She mutters, "I don't want to go on this vacation. It's boring."

"Okay, what would you like to do on vacation?"

"I don't want to ride in the car all day with those nerds, and I don't want to go to museums and on tours."

"But what do you want to do?"

"Go to the beach. Lay out. Hike in the mountains. Not do everything with the family."

"If we built in some beach time and didn't drive a great distance, would you go along and be pleasant?"

Begrudgingly, "Yeah, if I have to."

What we're doing in the group is teaching the art of collaboration, rather than talking about the need for it. Parents realize they need to collaborate with teens but they may not know how, particularly if they come from a family in which negotiation didn't exist, where Dad said, "This is what we're going to do and you're going to like it!"

Sometimes I role play the skill of parent-child negotiation, taking both parts myself. Or I take the part of the parent and ask the group to take the role of the adolescent.

A second question may come up. "Well, I have a stepdaughter who constantly tells me how much more fun it was in her earlier family. I don't know what to say, and I end up mad and silent."

I may respond, "That must be frustrating. Has anyone else here experienced this situation?" Since the problem is specific rather than general, response is apt to be minimal. The effective facilitator must decide quickly whether or not an issue is general enough in the group experience to discuss. If it isn't, we have to develop polite ways of dealing with the question, perhaps by saying, "We don't seem to have enough group experiences and solutions here, so let's you and I talk about it at breaktime." We cannot allow parent education sessions to turn into group therapy sessions. I suspect most of us have sat in groups where the facilitator permitted one person's problems to consume group time. When this happens, our reaction is likely to be anger: not with the questioner, but with the facilitator for failing to put closure on the question and move on to group concerns.

I recall a three-week course I took on instilling self-esteem in children. During the first session, a parent went into a long, involved story about her child. The professor, a therapist, allowed herself to get drawn into the story for forty-five minutes. She shelved her other material, which was of interest to the group, in favor of one person's unique situation. Only two-thirds of the class returned the following week, and when the professor permitted a repeat of the situation, she lost the class. Only a few returned for the final session. And we wished we hadn't.

Parent education is not group therapy. Parents may ask personal questions, but the facilitator decides whether the question is of sufficient general interest to discuss. One way of doing this is to check it out with the group: "Is this a common problem?" If they remain noncommittal, we need to identify the issue as requiring a one-on-one rather than group response.

I look for what I call the "nod index." If the issue is familiar and vexing to parents, they will nod when I ask, "Is this a common problem?" If I am still uncertain, I will ask, "How many of you experience this as a frustration? Please raise your hands." If few do, I offer an empathetic look at the questioning parent and say, "We need to move on, but I know how important this is to you, so let's talk about it privately later."

Sometimes the group surprises me, especially when I determine an issue to be insignificant but they don't. The first time I worked with military families in Germany, one parent went on at length about the school bus situation. "School bus?" I thought skeptically. In light of their other problems, such as family separation, drugs, and the like, I relegated her complaints to those of an unusually protective parent. Fortunately, I asked the group, "Is this problem frustrating most of you?"

"Yes," they responded emphatically. In listening to them, I discovered that the lengthy and unsupervised bus rides their children experienced daily led to behavior problems such as obscene language, pornography, and vandalism. On the spot, I judged the issue to be of paramount and general interest, not just one parent's obsession. We turned the discussion into one of powerlessness versus control. Were they as powerless to change the school bus situation as they felt? If they were in charge, what would they change? Not being in charge, how could they influence those in charge?

Out of this came several action-oriented proposals: They would, as a group, request monitors on the buses; if that didn't work, they would volunteer in pairs to ride the bus one day each month to monitor behavior; they would request support-system personnel, such as chaplains and family counselors, to assume some responsibility for monitoring bus conditions. The irony is that I never intended to discuss school bus behavior in a session on family stress, but when I found it of such vital interest, I shelved my golden words of wisdom and went with their issue. Results? That session earned the best evaluation of any of my presentations to parents in Europe.

Knowing when to go with group issues becomes easier with experience, but being able to depart from prepared material is the first courageous step. We all have pangs of resentment—I've prepared this wonderful lecture and I'm not going to be able to deliver it—but if we truly believe that the agenda arises from the parents, we have to be able to shelve our content or at least condense it to address the issues parents perceive as important.

In the usual one-and-a-half hour slot set aside for a parent session, we can address five or more issues. We don't have to set aside a question period because questions arise throughout the empowerment process. When parents leave, they feel both valued and informed. Often they will ask for another session. Recently I processed a group of adults on their personal faith development.

My opening question was, "At what point in your life did your faith take a leap ahead?" and my follow-up, "At what point did you experience a faith crisis?" We filled the charts, and then I offered a mini-lecture on the stages of faith development.

By the time I finished they had been sitting for over an hour, so I said, "Let's take a break." With unanimous voice, they said, "No, let's go on." They were so involved with the topic they were afraid a break would destroy the momentum. So I acceded to the group and continued (although *I* wanted a break). I am convinced that had I delivered the same material by lecturing and then asking for questions, they would have wanted a break and perhaps would have left during it.

This same process can be used effectively in one-on-one parent conferences. A social worker visiting a home might sit at a table with a parent, sipping a cup of coffee, and then pull out a sheet of paper and say, "Let's talk about what you like most about Tim," jotting down the responses: "He's funny. He asks me how I'm feeling. He's really a good kid, but . . ."

Here's where we interrupt and say, "No, we'll get to what you don't like in a minute. Let's just talk about what you like about him for now." And we continue with the process in the same way as with the group.

Teachers who use the process may begin by asking the parent of a child who isn't doing well in school, "What are some things Liz is good at?" By asking parents to identify strengths, we don't have to search for them and point them out to parents. Rather, parents point them out to us.

Do's and Don'ts of the Empowerment Process

While I am a supporter of the empowerment process in parenting and other forms of adult education, there are some pitfalls. To avoid these, let's discuss the do's and don'ts of some specific issues. The first two I have already mentioned, but I will repeat them for quick reference.

   1. The facilitator gets off the pedestal early.

   2. The agenda and solutions arise from the group or, in one-on-one situations, from the parent.
Now for some others.

   3. Content lies chiefly with the facilitator. This rule presumes we, as facilitators, have a plan or an agenda before we begin the session. We may not complete it, but it's there to use if we need it. In the example of the process I gave earlier, I was prepared to discuss separation identity, teen development, and parent-teen communication. I ended up teaching all three during the session, but I taught them in five-minute segments, rather than in a well-developed lecture.

The empowerment process does not mean that we don't need to be prepared. Effective facilitators prepare more material than lecturers generally do, because we don't know what topics will emerge. The chief fear parent educators express in moving from lecture to process is that of being found ignorant on a topic. We need not be afraid to say, "I'm sorry, but I am not familiar with the issue of homosexuality in the family or with the social development of emotionally handicapped children. I simply don't have any expertise or experience in these areas." If I feel the topic is important to the group, I may turn it over for group response, but that is a decision that I, as facilitator, must make. If the topic is of limited group interest, I may offer to research materials for the parent who asked the question.

Facilitators gain credibility when we admit ignorance on specific topics. Parents don't expect us to know everything. They do, however, sense and resent pretended knowledge. Of course, we can't say "I don't know" to everything. As facilitators, we are expected to be knowledgeable in our area. For example, teachers of first graders know what six-year-olds are like. They are educated in the emotional, motor, cognitive, and social development of six-year-olds. If they aren't knowledgeable, they shouldn't be teaching them. Fortunately, most first-grade teachers are well versed in this knowledge, so they should feel qualified and comfortable in facilitating a session with parents on "Enjoying Your Six-Year-Old." Very little is likely to emerge in the group that hasn't already emerged in class at one time or another.

A pediatrician or pediatric nurse is well versed in child wellness and illness and should not be afraid to process a group of parents who may have many questions that would go unanswered in a lecture session. Social workers, religious educators, child care providers, and recreation directors all have expertise in their given areas and are qualified to facilitate a group of parents without bringing in an "expert." But we have to recognize that we have these qualifications. If we don't, others will not.

4. The facilitator is responsible for controlling the agenda and the empowerment process. When the process breaks down, it is usually due to lack of control by the person in charge. The facilitator either allows the group to become monopolized by one or more parents, permits the session to veer into areas unrelated to the promised topic, or allows the group to deteriorate into a personal therapy session—occasionally someone will join a parenting session expecting it to be a sensitivity group where deep feelings are shared in hopes of group healing. When any of these happen, other members of the group begin to feel resentful and angry. The effective facilitator learns to perceive unrest and resentment in the group and then to tighten control, perhaps by saying, "I sense the group is ready to get back to the topic. Am I right?" Nods or the lack thereof verify or counter our suspicion. If there is group unrest, it is easy to say, "Okay, then let's get back to the issue of why children lie to parents."

I lost a group once in my early days of processing when I permitted two angry parents to turn the session from a discussion of the moral development of children into a discussion of why the Catholic church had changed. I allowed them to voice their feelings on ecumenism, nuns who don't wear habits, and a myriad of other issues unrelated to the stages at which children are able to deal morally with issues such as sharing toys, shoplifting, and teenage sex.

Today, if that happens in a group, I take control by saying, "Change in the Catholic church is an interesting topic to many, but that's not what we came together to discuss, so I'm going to move on to this item on the flip chart. Is this okay with the rest of you?" Grateful nods from the many will take the steam out of the few and the pressure off the facilitator.

Occasionally, a group tries to turn the process into an opportunity to vent frustrations at the system or to make scapegoats of administrators, clergy, or other leaders. When this happens, I usually allow them to vent for a short period and then say, "Okay, now that we've had a chance to vent, let's move on to ways of dealing with these frustrations."

When I was invited to facilitate a session on stress with a group of first sergeants in Korea, I began by bringing out of the group the positives and negatives of separation from their families. When we reached the negatives, a great deal of anger at the military system emerged. I realized that they needed an opportunity to vent their private feelings publicly, especially to a nonmilitary person. But I also knew I couldn't allow the seminar to degenerate into a three-hour gripe session. So, after twenty minutes of complaints, I said, "I think we have a pretty good idea of frustrations now. Let's take the major ones and focus on which are controllable and on how we can minimize the stress they engender." Group members were agreeable to the move and cooperated in going beyond complaints.

Another cause of group breakdown comes when our material is either too simple or too complex for the group. Boredom results when it's too simple, blank looks and muteness when it's too complex. If you sense either of these reactions setting in, gear your material up or down. I usually say, "This is too complex to get into right now. Let's move to the issue of . . ." or "I suspect you already know this so let's skip it and talk about . . ." More difficult to deal with is a group that is split in ability and training. What is appropriate for part of the group is too complex for the rest. As in any teaching situation, we have to find the middle ground between the two so that some participants have to stretch their minds more than they expected, while others have to accept less challenge than they may have wished.

If there is great diversity in the group, the session has not been well planned or appropriately publicized; for example, when I'm invited to direct a staff seminar on "Working Effectively with Parents" and planners invite parents to attend as well. It is almost impossible to talk about parent behaviors when parents are in attendance (or teen behaviors when teens are in attendance). Although I stipulate that the seminar is for those who *work* with parents, planners sometimes ignore my wishes in order to swell numbers. When this happens, I say at the outset, "This is a session on working with parents, not on parenting, so those of you who are expecting parenting help will be disappointed. You may want to leave. I don't want to take the chance of offending you when we start talking about some typical parent behaviors that drive teachers and other staff members crazy." This approach warns them and also gives them an opportunity to leave gracefully.

Finally, groups can fail if we insist upon laying our value system on parents. This action justifies one of the most common criticisms of parent education. If we try to sell a Puritan work ethic to a group of parents who do not view work as their primary goal or measurement of success in life, we are negating their value system. If we allow our attitudes toward working mothers, yearly pregnancies, religious behavior, serial marriages, or school attendance to influence our teaching, we are bound to fail with groups who will sense that we are not there to help them be more effective parents in their milieu, but to change *them* into *us*. We must avoid this temptation fiercely. It will arise when a parent says, "I want my son to quit school and get a job to help the family." Everything within us may shout, "No, don't do that." But if we respect parents we will turn the question into a learning opportunity by asking the group, "Okay, let's look at the situation. What are the advantages in his quitting school? The disadvantages?" By listing them, we are bringing responses out of the group rather than judging the parent with our value system.

The group always comes first. Being in control primarily means learning to deal effectively with problem participants, so I devote Chapter 6 to this topic.

Occasionally I am asked by participants if, by teaching the empowerment process as the most effective form of parent education, I object to developed programs like *STEP (Systematic Training for Effective Parenting)*, *Responsive Parenting*, *Active Parenting*, and *Positive Parenting*. Not at all. I endorse and recommend these programs for ongoing parent education. I've found that most of the commercial parenting programs embrace the process technique, often called the "empowering parents" method. The only caution I have with any program is that facilitators must feel free to be flexible, to move away from the material if they feel that the group is not responding. Inflexibility can doom any parent education effort. Programs are developed to serve us; we aren't required to serve them.

5. Humor is valuable in bonding the group and defusing tension. I find humor to be a most useful resource in working with parents. Participants, however, will wait for the facilitator to initiate humor. Many opportunities arise. Usually, responses to the opening question present an opportunity for a light moment, as when I asked a group to supply the ending to the statement, "I know I am stressed when . . ." Someone responded, "I can't eat." As one who battles weight, I stared at her and said, "Really. How does one get to that point?" Laughter followed, and I asked, "Does anyone have a different eating pattern with stress?" Several said they couldn't stop eating. It was a perfect opportunity for a mini-lecture on the relationship between stress and early eating habits. If I had simply listed "can't eat" and continued, we would have missed an opportunity for humor and for relief to those who overeat during times of stress.

As valid as humor is to the process, however, it must be controlled or the session becomes entertainment rather than education. People may enjoy it, but they won't learn what they came to learn. I once heard an adult say of a workshop, "It was great fun, but I honestly can't say I got anything out of it."

6. Positive precedes negative, and strengths precede stresses. People may get depressed when our first focus is on problems. They know their problems; they live with them; they experience them daily. They have not come to hear about their problems, but for help and support in dealing with them. When I'm asked to do a session on family stress, I begin with a handout on family *strengths* and stresses (see Appendix D), inviting participants first to select the strengths that would go to the top of the list in their family. Only after that do we discuss stresses.

The best method of establishing a positive atmosphere is to begin with an opening question that emphasizes the positive: "What do you like best about being married? Having two careers in your family? Having a two-year-old? (This takes a little thought.)" I devote considerable thought to my opening question because it sets the stage for the whole session. Eventually we will spend most of our time on problems and solutions, but we are far more effective if we begin with strengths and controllables.

One time I was invited to facilitate a session on school improvement that promised to be heated. We began by listing what attendees liked about the school system. Administrators and school board members in attendance, who had arrived with understandable defensiveness, were surprised to hear so many positives expressed. These disarmed both them and the parents, who reflected that, indeed, the school system was doing an effective job in many areas. I am convinced that the resulting discussion was more rational and conciliatory than it would have been had we started with complaints.

7. Handouts and simple outlines are helpful in hooking parents into the process; follow-up materials and information help sustain interest. I often use one or more handouts near the beginning of a session to entice parents to reflect on the given topic as it relates to their family. For example, if I use the handout on the family life cycle (Appendix E) or the one on methods of dealing with conflict (Appendix F), I'm providing parents with an easy method for taking notes. Handouts also serve to help participants recall information they can discuss later with a spouse or children not in attendance. However, we can overdo handouts. People get overwhelmed by too much paper. One or two handouts per session is more effective than many. We must also withhold the temptation to provide handouts on unrelated subjects just because we have them or have written them. Parents will gaze at the handouts with mystification, thinking, "What has this got to do with anything?"

I find it valuable to carry with me handouts and photocopies on specific topics, such as sharing responsibility in the home (Appendix G) and balancing the family's use of time (Appendix H), which I do not distribute but make available to interested parents. If the issue comes up, I say, "I have a handout that might be helpful on this. I'll put some on the table, and those who are interested can take one."

Follow-up is a valuable part of any parent education effort. We should view a class or workshop as a mere kickoff to the much longer game parents must play. Since we are resource people to parents, we should consider having materials and information available for them: books, cassette tapes, leaflets, packets, toys and games, information on future workshops, field trips, videos, suggested films and television offerings—anything that will help them extend their interest in parenting beyond our classroom.

8. *Professional jargon distances us from parents.* Because we talk with each other daily as professionals, we tend to converse in professional language: "motor development," "standard deviation," "pubescent peer interaction." Since parents don't use these terms, when we do we put a barrier between them and us that implies, "I am an authority because I use this language." Often we don't intend to intimidate parents, but when we use terminology that is familiar to us and not to them, it creates a barrier to openness.

I once sat in on a conference of family scholars who used "marital dyad" for couple and "marital triad" for couple and child. Although all of us who attended understood the terms, the constant use of them was grating and eventually became a joke among us.

My rule when working with parents is that if we can say it more simply, we should do so. All of us are capable of impressing clients with language, but it is counterproductive in our work with parents. If, in the heat of discussion, we unintentionally use technical language, we can catch ourselves and be forgiven by parents by saying, "I am really impressing myself today, aren't I? All this phrase means is . . ." and putting it into familiar language. I once heard a speaker respond to a parent's question with "You are symmetrically escalating the interaction," instead of "You are heating up the fight."

The more impressive the audience, the more we tend to reach for professional jargon. Academia, religion, education, medicine, psychology, sociology—each has its own language that parents may understand but do not feel comfortable using. Contrary to what we might like to believe, we don't impress parents with erudite language as much as we offend them.

Because I write a weekly column on parenting, I have to be careful to use language easily understood by readers. I keep a small plaque above my desk to remind me to keep my terminology simple. Unfortunately, it doesn't credit an author, but it goes like this:

> And Jesus said,
> "Who do you say I am?"
> And they answered,
> "You are the eschatological
> manifestation of the ground
> of our being, the kerygma
> in which we found the
> ultimate meaning of our
> interpersonal relationship."
> And Jesus said,
> "*What?*"

9. Controversial attitudes on the part of the facilitator diminish effectiveness; it's the facilitator's responsibility to handle controversy objectively. In recent years, the family has become a moral and political issue, so controversies continue to emerge. There are many parents who feel it is immoral for mothers to work, moral for parents to spank, and so on. These issues are likely to arise in a group, but the effective facilitator learns to handle them objectively. I am not implying that we must conceal our own attitudes, but that we not express them immediately. A comment that husbands should share household chores equally will serve as a red flag to many parents, men and women alike. Their irritation may prevent them from hearing anything further we may have to say.

However, if the issue arises later on, perhaps when a woman indicates frustration over being left alone in the kitchen after dinner to do the cleanup, I may say, "Well, I happen to believe that when both spouses put in eight-hour days they should share household responsibilities. We do in our family, but I realize others don't agree with this. The question we need to consider is not whether it is proper or improper for husbands to help but, if the issue is causing stress in the family, how it can be addressed."

Occasionally during the process, someone will respond to a problem posed by a parent with, "Well, all your kid needs is a good whipping." Some listeners will nod in agreement, while others recoil in horror. It is best for the facilitator to respond, "Spanking is a controversial issue among parents. Some feel it is a parental responsibility, while others feel it is wrong. Let's not get into the morality of spanking here, but only the effectiveness of it. How many of you were spanked as children?" Hands go up. "Okay, let's list the advantages and disadvantages of spanking."

I turn to the always-ready flip chart, which usually ends up looking like this:

Advantages	Disadvantages
Stops bad behavior.	Makes child worse.
Shows I'm boss.	Makes me feel guilty.
Makes me feel better.	Tells child hitting is okay.
Teaches a lesson.	I can get out of control.
	Makes my kids scared of me.
	Kids get too big to spank.
	They can hate you for life.
	They will spank my grandchildren.

The list broadcasts the message that disadvantages outweigh advantages. We don't need to moralize, just let parents draw their own conclusions. If we follow this with, "What are some alternatives to spanking?" and list them, we are giving parents ideas and permission to reach for alternative methods for correcting behavior.

The empowerment process will degenerate into meaningless and endless argument if we permit deeply held attitudes to take over. We can put closure on an emotional and controversial issue with a simple comment like, "Remember, we don't have to defend our right to our opinions, even if others disagree. Let's get on with the stresses of women who work outside the home and those who stay home."

10. The process should be abandoned if it isn't working. Occasionally, even the best facilitators will encounter a group that, for some reason, refuses to engage in the process. No matter how many different opening questions we offer, the group sits mutely. I don't always know why this happens. Perhaps it's the chemistry of a given group. Perhaps it's due to the resentment caused by forced attendance; participants mutely agree to punish the facilitator for their having to attend. This situation happened to me once when I was invited to a large hospital to present a session on family stress with resident physicians. They resolutely refused to say anything, even when I changed the opening question from personal stress to "What signs of stress do you perceive in your patient families?"

After fifteen minutes of trying to crack the stone faces in front of me, I sensed resentment and deliberate sabotage, so I stopped trying to involve them and turned to my lecture notes. Gradually, they loosened up. Some even took notes, and one apologized privately to me later for the group's resistance. It was then that I learned that in order to practice in that hospital, physicians were mandated to attend a certain number of hours of personal inservice training annually. My session happened to be the last offered that calendar year, so those who had put it off were my attendees. Their lack of cooperation was their way of showing contempt for the requirement and of embarrassing the hospital administrators who were my hosts.

The facilitator in situations like this is victimized, but not helpless. If a group won't talk, we, as facilitators, can. We simply turn to the lecture format. I know some facilitators who refuse invitations that require participant attendance, such as sessions for court-ordered parents, hospital-ordered physicians, or super-intendent-ordered teachers. I don't refuse these invitations, but I quickly abandon the process if the attendees are uncooperative.

Another mute situation can arise when there is a clear hierarchy in the group, with the chief in attendance—military officers whose commander is sitting in the front row, or priests whose bishop attends the session. Participants are understand-ably less likely to admit to problems or to vent frustrations when they fear reprisal.

Fortunately, these difficult occasions rarely occur with parents. In ten years, I have had only three such experiences, and the only one involving parents was with a roomful of court-ordered parents. After several futile attempts to get them to respond, I simply shelved the process and began talking about how parents can deal effectively and ineffectively with troublesome children.

A good facilitator should not be afraid to admit to a group that an exercise has flopped. Members already suspect it, and our trying to cover it up merely increases the flop. Maybe a role-play exercise doesn't work out or a small-group task comes up empty-handed. Simply remark to the group, "I'm sorry we took time for this because it didn't work out the way I had hoped. I did learn one thing—to file it in my wastebasket." They will laugh and respect us for admitting fallibility.

Remember, the lecture format is always there for us to use if the empowerment process doesn't work. But, since I prefer having parents make the decision about their participation, I like to begin with the process.

Chapter *5*

When Lecture We Must . . .

As much as we may prefer the empowerment process to other forms of parent education, there are times that call for a lecture format. When a group numbers over sixty, the empowerment process is largely ineffective. When a topic doesn't touch the personal experience of most parents in the audience—AIDS or suicide, for example—we are unable to process solutions from the group. When the topic demands step-by-step instruction, as in preparing a workable family budget, the lecture format is more useful than the empowerment process.

If we are working with participants who are uncomfortable with speaking out in a group, the process won't work. Years ago, I tried without much success to use the process with a group of Native American mothers. Later, I commented to my hostess, herself a Native American home economist, that the women seemed uninterested. "Not at all," she replied. "Our people are taught that if you voice a solution or mention a success, it diminishes the value of other people in the group." If I had been aware of their cultural values, I would not have attempted the process. Now I ask about the group's traditions and mores before I plan a session.

Lectures can be exciting or dull. Most of us have experienced both kinds. Some forethought and research can make all the difference when we plan a lecture for a specific group. Some strategies to consider when preparing a lecture are:

*1. **Use a good hook.*** "Hook" is a writer's term for the opening of an article. It has a literal translation: we want to grab (hook) the reader's interest immediately so he or she won't turn the page and bypass our words. Many lecturers ignore the need for a hook and launch immediately into the material. When we do this, we miss a good opportunity for bonding, humor, and immediate stimulus. When preparing a lecture, select a technique for hooking listeners that best fits your topic. Your hook may even serve as a framework for your presentation. Some suggestions:

- Quote: "Will Rogers once said, 'I never made a mistake, partly because I never made a decision.' Some of us who work with families are tempted at times to follow his example. It's sometimes easier to accept policies than to challenge them. . . ."
- Anecdote or joke: "Thank you for that generous introduction and warm reception. It takes the sting out of the comment from the woman who told me she was reading my column for Lent."
- Personal experience: "I'd like to use a personal experience to launch our topic today. I was thirty-six when I had my youngest child. The woman in the hospital room with me was eighteen. The first words she said to me were, 'My mother is your age.'"
- Statistic: "According to statistics, every day in our country, 210 Americans reach the age of 100. Who is parenting them?"
- Question: "What would you do if your fifteen-year-old daughter came to you and said, 'Mom, I think I'm pregnant'? Would you cry? Shout with joy, 'I'm going to be a grandmother'? Would you throw her out? Would you ask for more information? Few parents know what they would do until the occasion arises."
- National news event localized: "Millions of Americans found a new hero in Oliver North during the summer of 1987. But polls indicate that while they loved him, they deplored his tactics. Why the dichotomy? When we talk about family value systems, the Oliver North phenomenon is a good place to start."
- Local news event generalized: "Our community suffered eleven teenage suicides last year. We grieve and wonder, 'Is it our community alone?' No, it isn't. The problem of adolescent loss of hope is a national one that needs to be addressed in every home, school, and community in America."

2. *Keep your topic specific and manageable.* Researchers and academicians are trained to follow several trains of thought simultaneously and to make connections between them. Most other people aren't skilled in doing so. When working with parents, I find it most effective to select a specific topic, such as

"Helping Children Deal with Insecurity," and stay with it, tempting as it may be to stray into related areas like birth order and historical forms of parenting. Parents, for the most part, don't really care about the evolution of parenting, although the subject may fascinate us. One of the most familiar lecture evaluation comments is, "The speaker rambled." Often the speaker hasn't rambled but has failed to make a clear connection between background information and its application to the topic.

I find that parents respond well to enumerated points, steps, or principles in a lecture. They pick up their pencils when I say, "There are four categories of family stress I want to address. The first is . . ." If you use this technique, be careful not to spend too much time on the first point or listeners will get nervous, thinking they are going to be captive listeners for hours. Allocate a certain number of minutes to each point and stick to your timetable.

3. Use lots of anecdotes. Anecdotes emphasize a point more effectively than does general content. I try to give some specific information and then explain it with a story. For example, in a session on setting limits and consequences, I may say, "If at all possible, tie the consequence to the behavior or offense. If the child resists getting up when called in the morning and it becomes a matter of ongoing family stress, say sympathetically to the child that you realize she needs more sleep, so for a week there will be an earlier bedtime. This takes the issue out of the punishment realm and puts it into an empathetic and caring framework." Then I will tell the story of the mother who, when her child hit a sibling, said, "I see the violence of television is rubbing off on you. Let's cancel TV for you for the next two days and see if it helps you stop hitting." Parents will remember the television story longer than my comments on linking misbehavior and consequences.

Be careful, however, to limit your anecdotes to those that emphasize your point. If, in a moment of abandonment, you begin telling stories that have little relevance to your point, parents may become puzzled and wonder, "What does this have to do with the topic?"

4. Weave essential, but less interesting, content into the whole of your lecture. Some basic content—statistics, history, background, theory—is necessary for a good lecture, but it doesn't have to come at the beginning when people are not yet hooked on your topic, style, qualifications, or enthusiasm. I am often surprised by teachers and lecturers who begin with, "Back in 1930, the Commission on . . ." or "I want to begin by citing achievement statistics of preschool children in various parts of the country over the past ten years." A sure way to let ennui set in. Instead, use a good hook and follow with why the topic is of interest to you and of value to listeners. Then go into your basic points and intersperse your content with anecdotes. You will find listeners alert and responsive.

5. Try to involve your audience by asking them to respond. Even if we can't process a group because of its size, it helps to enlist participants as active listeners by asking a question that elicits general response. I often ask, "Who here has teens at home?" When they raise their hands, I say, "Good. Now, can somebody give me a typical nonverbal response exhibited by teens?" Someone from the audience may say, "The slammed door." Another comments, "Rolling their eyes." This participation gives parents the feeling that they have something to offer, and they enjoy the interchange.

6. Cite specific books and programs that might be helpful as follow-up. State titles and authors slowly and then repeat the information so it can be written down. Too often, lecturers make quick references that only mystify and irritate listeners. Who hasn't been annoyed by a comment such as, "The best work on this topic is Gesell's, and I suggest you pick that up. Others, of course, are Piaget and Bronfenbrenner. . . ." To parents this is intimidating and frustrating. They may perceive it as lecturer conceit: "Look how much I know that you don't."

7. Tie your tag or conclusion into your hook. People like a sense of completeness. After you have delivered your lecture, tie up the pieces with a short summary, a bit of hope, and a reference to your opening hook. There are several ways of tying the hooks I suggested at the beginning of this chapter into your tag or ending:

- Quote: "Will Rogers may have made it through life without making a decision, but few parents are able to do so. We make decisions daily, some good, some poor. But that's part of parenting. And lucky is the child whose parents aren't afraid to make decisions."
- Anecdote or joke: "I appreciate your attention and response. I hope you don't leave here feeling like the woman who was reading my column for Lent—as if you had endured undue penance."
- Personal experience: "In closing, let me go back to the young mother in my hospital room. Although we were of different generations, we both had new babies who would grow up in the same era. That was, and is, our common denominator.

We all are parents, and we have much to learn from each other, regardless of our age and experience."
- Statistic: "We may not have parents who will be numbered among the 210 elderly who daily reach the age of 100, but parenting the older generation, whatever its age, has its rewards and stresses. Let's begin to focus on the rewards and learn to deal with the stresses."
- Question: "We may never have to face the question of what we would do if our fifteen-year-old told us she was pregnant. But many parents do. Our reaction to and support for those parents will make a significant difference in how they view themselves as parents."
- National news event localized: "I suspect that in five years, few of us will remember the name Oliver North, especially not our children. There will be new public figures. But, as we've learned from history, values are ageless, and we will still be struggling to retain values within the family."
- Local news event generalized: "Our community lost eleven teenagers, yes. But we didn't lose the 4,300 who remain in our midst and in our schools. They are still here, looking for hope and dreaming of life. We can be models of hope for them if we believe in our power to make a difference."

8. *Deal with questions as succinctly as possible.* When you have a large audience, fielding questions is difficult. If you do take questions from the floor, be sure to repeat them so all can hear. It's annoying to have to play the Guess-the-Question game while listening to the answer. Don't spend too much time on a given question if there are other people waiting to ask questions. If a question requires too elaborate a response, invite the questioner to stop at the lectern after you have finished.

What do you do if you ask for questions and none come? Prime the pump. Say, "Earlier today someone asked me about . . ." or "A question I am frequently asked is . . ." Or, better yet, accept that people have sat long enough and are ready to leave. Say, "I think you need to stretch now. If any of you have questions, please come up and I'll try to answer them for you."

I like to stay around after a lecture, because some people who have valid questions are timid about asking them in a group. If one person monopolizes the speaker, others who are waiting may get edgy. To offset this, I say, "Let me answer these others, and I'll get back to you." It usually serves notice on the acceptable and considerate amount of time a questioner should consume.

One final caution: If you are an effective lecturer, word will get around, and you will receive many invitations to speak. It's tempting (and easy) to deliver the same lecture repeatedly, but try not to become a one-speech lecturer. A reaction you don't want from parents and professionals is, "I've already heard her." Rather, you want to hear, "She always has something worthwhile to say."

This means, of course, constant study and research on your part so that you have new ideas, insights, and skills to impart, regardless of the number of times someone has heard you speak. The exception to this emerges if you are asked by planners to deliver the same lecture to another audience in a different geographical or professional area. When I presented a lecture on "Work and Family" to a large national convention, I received many invitations to repeat the lecture in other states. Planners were insistent that my presentation be identical to the lecture they had heard. "I want our people to hear what you said," they told me. So I repeated that lecture eight times.

In summary, lectures need not intimidate us nor bore our listeners. When we hook parents' attention, show enthusiasm for the topic, offer relevant information and interesting anecdotes, and engage participants in what we have to offer, they will respond positively. They may even ask for more.

Chapter *6*

Dealing with Problem Parents

Just as teachers face problem students and social workers face problem families, so do parent educators find potential problem parents in a group—probably the same ones who were problem kids, in fact. Because problem participants show up in all kinds of adult education groups, this chapter applies to anyone who stands in front of adult groups, be they college teachers or management executives.

When I discussed this section with my daughter, who is in graduate school, she said, "Mom, I wish every college professor would read this." Why? Because an audience loses respect for the teacher or facilitator who relinquishes control of a class or group by allowing individuals in the audience to dominate. We must remember that the group looks to the leader for control of agenda and participants alike.

Curtailing participants who hamper group discussion does not mean we have to be unkind, but simply that we need to learn diplomatic ways of remaining firmly in control. Although participants may not like the behavior of a fellow member, they feel uncomfortable when the facilitator is unkind or rude. To avoid being thought rude or mean, some facilitators operate under a covenant of niceness. They allow one or two participants to go on endlessly with theories or stories that have little relevance to the topic.

For those new to facilitating, let me emphasize that control gets easier with experience. In the beginning we may be overly accommodating in an effort to be liked. Eventually, we learn to disagree diplomatically. Some useful phrases for responding to distractions or argumentative comments are:

"I don't happen to agree with you, but . . ."
"I wish I could go along with you on that, but . . ."
"I'm afraid my experience doesn't reflect yours . . ."
"I don't want us to get distracted by that right now . . ."

When we adopt this manner of response, we are respectful both to the individual and to the group. We state our own opinions and expectations while preserving the individual's dignity.

I once began a session with army chaplains with some assumptions about young enlistees. When I reached my fourth assumption, one chaplain said, "I don't know where you're getting these. My men aren't like this at all." Because there had been a great deal of affirmation of my assumptions in the group, I turned it over to them, saying, "These are only assumptions, not facts. Am I assuming incorrectly? Are these valid assumptions in your experience?" They nodded and said "yes" vigorously. So I said, "When I state assumptions and they don't correlate with your experience, please disregard them. If they are valid, consider them." Then I turned to the dissenting chaplain and said, "Let's look at why most of the chaplains here relate to these assumptions, but you can't."

It took only a moment to discover that the troops with whom the dissenting chaplain worked were older and more highly educated than the average enlistee. He was correct in challenging my assumptions, but he readily discovered that his was a unique situation. He said, "I'm sorry. I didn't realize the extent of these problems." "Don't apologize," I replied. "I'm pleased you felt comfortable enough to challenge me and the group. It helps us clarify the diversity of those you face."

In an earlier time, I probably would have been intimidated by his question, and perhaps would have apologetically withdrawn my assumptions. But experience teaches us to deal with dissent. If the group had agreed with him, I would have said, "Let's shelve my assumptions and consider yours. Why do you believe your young enlistees lower their values so quickly when they come overseas?"

Some facilitators get unduly upset over problem participants, but there are ways of dealing effectively with them. All it takes is a little knowledge and practice. I have categorized several types of disrupters and offer specific techniques to use with each type in retaining control over the group.

Monopolizing Morris. Morris likes to talk. He responds the minute there is a pause. He must be stopped or he will monopolize

and irritate the group to the point that they will roll their eyes
every time he begins, and ultimately remain silent themselves.
The group expects the facilitator to control Morris, and if he isn't
silenced, the group may become angry and disappointed. How
do we handle Morris? We don't make eye contact with him. We
don't see his raised hand. If he doesn't get the point, we refer to
the one-comment-per-person rule stated earlier in the class or
session: "Wait a minute, Morris. Everybody gets to talk once before
anybody gets to talk twice. Does anyone else want to say
something on this?" The group usually cooperates by quickly
becoming vocal. We then can ignore Morris and move on.

Assisting Archie. Archie is intrusive. He tries to take over
leadership of the group by suggesting, "Wouldn't it be better if
we . . ." or "I've got an idea. Why don't we . . ." He may leaf
through your notes at the podium or change the furniture around
to his liking during break. Archie's problem is that he wants to
be the facilitator, or he wants recognition and approval. Archies
don't come full-grown. Elementary teachers learn early that junior
Archie wants attention and approval, so they respond by giving
him tasks. In a parenting group, we can put Archie to work for
us. We can ask him to distribute the handouts, tell us when it's
time for a break, reconvene the group, check the thermostat, open
windows, and close doors. When Archie is given these responsibilities, he is usually happy with his role and stops intruding on
facilitator turf.

Harmonizing Holly. Holly is the pourer of oil on troubled
waters. She can't stand tension. When there is disagreement she
says, "Oh, I'm sure he didn't mean that," or "I think you two are
really saying the same thing." Since disagreement is an integral
part of good discussion, we have to control Holly, or her inability
to deal with tension will discomfit the whole group. We handle
Holly by saying, "It's okay, Holly. Remember, we can disagree and
still respect and like each other." This relieves Holly's anxiety and
gives the group permission to continue to disagree. Sometimes I
use a Holly situation to introduce conflict resolution techniques,
saying, "Some of you seem uncomfortable whenever we begin to
disagree. Let's stop a minute and talk about ways of dealing with
conflict in families and in groups. It may help us here as well as
at home."

Peggy Perfect. Peggy is the perfect parent of perfect children,
and she can rapidly become Peggy Pain to the group. She believes
she has no problems and that those she has experienced in the

past she has dealt with perfectly. Peggy doesn't believe she needs parent education. Sometimes she attends because other people's problems make her feel better. Peggy is the one who will say, "We've never had an argument with our teenagers," or "If you just hug your children enough, they will do what you ask." Peggy stirs up fantasies of homicide in the group.

To be fair, some Peggys really are very good parents and are attending because they want to remain good. These are an asset in any group, because they are able to offer workable solutions to problems that arise. If we have only dysfunctional parents in a group, few successful techniques can be shared. Whether she be smug or humble, Peggy can be useful in dealing with the next two participants.

Suffering Sue Ann. Sue Ann is in pain all the time. She tends to tell long, sad, drawn-out stories with many detours. Because she is apt to be a chronic complainer, family and friends don't listen to her. She attempts to find relief in a class situation where she will be heard. Sue Ann can ruin a class. When she begins a tale of woe, others begin reading or their eyes harden as if they are groaning collectively, "Not again."

The facilitator is responsible for silencing Sue Ann. If there is a Peggy Perfect in the group, we can interrupt Sue Ann's long story and say, "How sad this must be for you, Sue Ann. We have to move on, but perhaps Peggy or others here have some ideas on how to handle your situation. Maybe you two can talk about this later." Actually, we are pairing one who needs to be listened to with one who needs recognition. We are meeting both needs.

If there isn't a Peggy in class, we can say gently, "I don't want to get into that now, but your problem is a familiar one. If anyone here has dealt with it, please talk with Sue Ann after the session and tell her how you handled it." We aren't ignoring Sue Ann as much as we are rescuing the group from her personal need to be heard. Remember, the group always comes first.

Wavering Winnie. Winnie has low self-esteem and tries to preserve what she has by rejecting solutions. She is the person frequently referred to by professionals as the "Yabba" ("Yeah, but that wouldn't work for me because . . ." and "Yeah, but I tried that once . . ."). Therapists tell us that Winnie doesn't want answers; she wants sympathy. Since we are not in a therapeutic setting, we must realize that we can't solve Winnie's problems as long as she continues rejecting our suggestions.

We have two choices with Winnie. We can counsel her privately (or turn her over to Peggy, as we did with Sue Ann) or we can confront her resistance by saying, "We've run out of solutions, Winnie, so unless you can come up with some additional ones, I guess you're going to have to learn to live with your situation." Winnie can be remarkably tenacious, consuming enormous amounts of group time while rejecting group help. By feeding her helplessness, we encourage her irresponsibility. If she persists, sometimes the only way to deal with her is to again confront her gently: "It doesn't sound like you want help, Winnie," or "I'm sorry. We've offered all we can. Maybe counseling would be more valuable for you than a class."

Isabel Interrupter. We may have a parent in the group who habitually interrupts speakers. Because most adults are too kind to deal openly with this annoyance, the facilitator must quickly and firmly stop it by saying, "Hold on, Isabel. I don't think she's finished." If Isabel is allowed to continue interrupting, the group will assume that interruptions are acceptable and will pick up the habit. If this happens, I say, "We seem to be getting into the habit of interrupting one another. I'm not comfortable with this. Are you?" If the facilitator diplomatically calls attention to an annoying group habit, it usually stops.

Clarence Clown. Clarence tries to make a joke out of everything, especially if the subject is a sensitive one for him. He jokes to cover up his feelings, to get the group off the subject, or simply to be liked by the group. Sometimes Clarence is funny, more often not.

I'm not talking here of the person who makes an occasional joke that is not at another's expense. These people are gems in a class. An example is the time my group talked of spouse-inspired guilt. I asked the women how they would respond if their husband came home from work while they were reading a magazine, immediately took out the sweeper, and started cleaning the carpet. One woman said, "I'll lift my feet for you, Honey." Her response delighted the group.

Clarence Clown, on the other hand, often makes jokes at inopportune times. He must be stopped for two reasons. One, he can encourage clones and turn the session into a "Can you top this?" show. Those of us who have taught high schoolers know how easily we can lose a class this way. Two, other people won't share if they're afraid their remarks will generate ridicule and laughter. Once, when we were discussing negotiating with children, a sincere young mother said, "What do I tell my eleven-year-old daughter who wants to pierce her ears and wear pantyhose? I think she's too young, but I don't know how to negotiate with her on this."

Clarence jumped in: "Let her pierce one ear and wear one stocking." (I warned you he wasn't always funny.) The mother recoiled with hurt. I said quickly, "Wait a minute, Clarence. This may be funny to you, but it's a very real issue with many of us. When do we allow our children to adopt grown-up behavior?" And I turned the question over to the group. If Clarence continues to clown after such facilitator reaction, we can talk with him privately at the break. "Her feelings were hurt by your comment, Clarence, and I don't want that to happen in my groups. Please be more sensitive in the future." If this doesn't stop him, we can say, "Not funny, Clarence," and let him experience the embarrassment he inflicts on others.

Shifting Sasha. Sasha changes the subject on you. Sometimes you wonder if you're even in the same room with her. Sometimes Sasha is just spacey, asking off-the-wall questions that cause facilitator and class alike to stop in midtopic and look around in puzzlement. Sasha is an example of what we call a scattered thinker. It's difficult for her to follow a line of thought because she is bombarded by diverse and seemingly unconnected thoughts of her own.

The best way to handle Sasha is to smile and say, "That's interesting, Sasha, but I'm going to put you on hold until we finish the topic we're on." She's usually happy with this because she's already into another subject. However, before we put her on hold, we need to ask her the connection between our topic and her question. She may see a connection we haven't seen, or she may simply need to articulate her question better.

I recall the time a group was discussing problems with grandparents, especially their tendency to overindulge grandchildren. Sasha raised her hand and said, "I really hate Ohio." The group's collective heads jerked up, mine included. "Sasha, I'm not sure I heard you right. Are you talking about Ohio?" I asked. "Yes," she said vigorously. "Whenever we visit my husband's parents in Dayton . . ." and she launched into a question directly related to the topic, although her original statement indicated no such relationship.

Sometimes Sasha deliberately shifts the topic, either to avoid it because it's sensitive or to introduce an unrelated topic she wants discussed. Politely but firmly, we must put her on hold. I usually say, "If we have time when we're finished with our topic, we'll go on to yours, Sasha."

Court-ordered Kirk. Kirk is the participant who doesn't want to be there. He may be court-ordered; that is, he cannot retain custody of his children unless he takes some parenting classes. He may be church- or school-ordered, and his child can't be enrolled unless he attends some sessions. Or, more likely, he may be spouse-ordered. Kirk can sabotage the class and intimidate the facilitator with his behavior. He adopts a permanent sneer, belligerent body language, and other sophomoric behavior. Still, I invite you to reflect on the times you were forced to attend a workshop or class. How did you respond to the facilitator's enthusiasm? With cooperation or with a stone face? A negative attendee like Kirk has power over an insecure facilitator. He can disrupt such a facilitator's confidence and agenda.

A common facilitator error lies in our tendency to focus on resistant participants rather than supportive ones. We find ourselves talking directly to the recalcitrants, trying to entice them into liking us and the group, striving unsuccessfully to get them to smile or nod in agreement. This strategy doesn't work, because a person like Kirk is delighted when we're nervous. He is out to punish someone for his forced attendance, and we are the visible target. I know of only one way to deal effectively with court-ordered participants, and that is to defuse them immediately. I say, "I know some of you don't want to be here, and I'm sorry you have to be. So feel free to sleep, daydream, or read. We'll try not to distract you."

Having acknowledged and dispatched them, we can then focus on positive participants. We need to turn our attention to those who are there willingly and give them what they came to learn. We must recognize the rule of thumb that we're going to please only 80 percent of any group at any time. If we focus on engaging the 20 percent, we're ignoring our support system.

I once had a parent group that included an angry, court-ordered father who took a seat in the back row and promptly turned his chair to the wall. I made my statement of sympathy to those who were forced to be in attendance and turned my attention to those who wanted to be in the group. As the session wore on and we got into much laughter over the behavior of children, this man's head began inching around. He strained to see other participants. His chair remained facing the wall throughout the evening, but his body had contorted to a double-jointed position by the time we ended. He bade me a face-saving goodbye, saying, "For a teacher, you weren't too bad." I took it as a high compliment.

Precocious Pamela. Pamela jumps in with a solution before the group senses the problem. Pamela has a tendency to be both impulsive and opinionated. A parent asks, "When should we ignore our son's temper tantrums?" "Never!" Pamela responds. If the facilitator doesn't step in, discussion will end there without addressing the parent's question or opening the group to solutions.

An effective response may be, "That's one answer. Do you all agree with Pamela?" If they shake their heads, ask, "When would you ignore a child's tantrum?" If the group is unresponsive, the facilitator might say, "I don't agree, Pamela. I think there are times when tantrums are best ignored. One is when . . ." Don't ignore Pamela's quick and often judgmental responses. They will stifle group interaction and intimidate others from free and open exchange. The group may be afraid to challenge Pamela, but they expect the facilitator to do so. Often when Pamela is challenged a few times, she will withdraw her quick, vocal judgments.

Fighting Frank. Frank enjoys a fight and argues with everybody. Some Franks are naturally abrasive and don't realize it, while other Franks are angry all the time. Whichever they are, you must protect victims from Frank. When he attacks a person's right to an opinion, the facilitator can say, "Hold on, Frank. We don't have to defend our right to an opinion here," or "This is a discussion, Frank, not a debate. What do you have to say about the topic?"

Frank tends to attack the speaker rather than the topic, so our task is to keep the discussion on the topic and prevent it from becoming a personal exchange. This is not to say that disagreement, a valuable part of group interaction, should be stifled. But disagreement should focus on the subject at hand, rather than · on personalities. Perhaps political campaigns can best illustrate this situation. Opposing candidates frequently begin by discussing a political issue like the arms race, but then degenerate into personal mudslinging and character assassination. The arms race issue gets lost in the name-calling.

A good way to deal with argumentative participants is to ask the group, "Do you want to spend time arguing about this or move on?" This strategy turns the issue over to the group and skirts

one-on-one confrontations that can destroy a session. Once in a
rare while, the facilitator who inherits a Frank may have to take
him aside during the break and say, "I don't know what's going
on, Frank, but I'm concerned about what your anger is doing to
the group. Please try to be more considerate of others," or "Please
cut back on the personal attacks, Frank. I'm a facilitator, not a
referee." If this doesn't stop him, ask him to leave the group. "I
don't think this is the group for you, Frank. It just makes you
angry, and people are reacting negatively. I think it's best if you
look around for a group more in line with your point of view."

I once encountered a female Frank who had just undergone a
particularly unpleasant divorce and held great anger toward
men, all men. Her contempt toward the men in our group was so
destructive I had to ask her to leave. It wasn't pleasant, but my
first responsibility was to the group, not to her need to vent her
anger, which was destroying the group. I suggested a support
group to her, one that encouraged women to vent their anger,
rather than a parenting group.

Punitive Pauline. Pauline is a punishing and moralistic person
who believes that parents who make mistakes are bad, that when
children grow up and get into trouble, it's because parents aren't
religious enough or rigid enough. Pauline's reactions often are
nonverbal, as in an audible catch-of-breath or shudder when a
parent admits striking a child in anger.

The most effective way of handling Pauline is to say, "Remember, Pauline, we aren't here to judge, but to learn." Then turn to
the parent: "What did you learn about yourself when you struck
your child?" I find it face-saving for Pauline's victims if I say
something like, "I've come close enough to striking my children
that I know how scary those feelings are," or "I'm glad I'm not the
only one who, in a fit of anger, has told my teenager to leave
home." Whether true or not, it relieves the victim's discomfort and
serves notice on Pauline to discontinue her punitive behavior.

With the increase in conflicting parenting methods in recent
years, the Paulines have become more abundant and vocal. If the
group is to have open discussion, we must respect Pauline's
opinions, while not permitting her to inflict her opinions on others.
A simple statement such as this often takes care of the situation:
"We all hold different beliefs on what's right and wrong, so out of
respect for all, we're not going to get into the morality of behavior.
Rather, we'll deal with practical ways of changing the behaviors
we don't like in ourselves and our children." If Pauline persists

by quoting Scripture or a popular evangelist, we can smile and say, "Thank you, Pauline. Now, on to the topic at hand . . ." We are neither agreeing nor disagreeing, ignoring nor confronting; we are listening and moving on.

Conceptualizing Conor. Conor has a theory for everything. Don't let him theorize you out of the group. If you encourage him, his theories—and the group's ennui—will grow. Eyes will roll heavenward when Conor begins, "Well, I have a theory on why today's kids . . ." Gently interrupt Conor with, "I'm sure your theory is interesting, Conor, but we want to finish this first. Why don't you stay around after class and discuss your theory with those who want to hear more about it?" Parents don't join a group to hear someone's theories. If they're forced to listen to them, they will leave at the first opportunity.

Carping Couple. This couple argues openly in the group, or one talks about the other in the third person, as in, "Well, what do you do if she spoils the kids all the time?" Spousal dissension causes anxiety in the group, and the facilitator must stop it. I resort to the earlier-stated rule, saying, "Sounds as if you two disagree on this, but remember, we can disagree and still like each other. Now let's look at the issue of spoiling and what it really means."

I try to turn the discussion from personal accusations to working together on the issue, but in so doing, I take it away from the couple and present it to the group: "Let's focus on spoiling for a minute. Have any of you ever been guilty of spoiling your children? Good. Let's make a list of things we've done when we spoiled our children:

- "said yes, when I wanted to say no"
- "gave in after they begged"
- "bought them something they didn't need"

If the couple attempts to return to their own unresolved agenda, the facilitator can gently but firmly say: "Let's deal with the issue you brought up. You can argue privately later when you're alone." This tells them that the group isn't interested in their ongoing antagonism. A parent education group is no place for marriage counseling, although the facilitator may privately suggest counseling to the couple.

Frequently, a question or discussion in the group alerts the facilitator to deep problems within a family, problems that a parenting class cannot address. What is the role of the facilitator in these instances? We must judge each situation carefully and

decide whether or not to suggest professional help, especially if
such help is unrequested. I prefer to err on the side of action
rather than inaction, but I always approach individuals privately.
I may approach them at the end of the session and say, "I was
reflecting on what you said about your son's behavior. It seems
more volatile than normal adolescent anger, and I think if I were
in your place, I'd check it out with someone. What do you think?"
For the most part, I have found parents to be grateful for my
raising the question, but I've had some who haven't wanted to
discuss it. With them, I don't push further, because parent
education is not therapy.

Pathological Patty. Patty is emotionally ill and needs a
therapy group rather than a class. She doesn't appear often in a
parenting group, but when she does, you will have no difficulty
recognizing her. An emotionally ill person can destroy a parenting
group, especially if she is innocently outspoken in her opinions.
She can hurt others deeply without realizing it.

Without being unkind, you need to let Patty know that the class
is not the place for her. "I don't think this is the best group for
you," a facilitator might say, "but I'll help you find one that you
will like better."

Readers need to keep in mind that not all the problem types
identified here emerge in a given group. It's unlikely that we will
face more than one or two problem participants in any group.
However, these are the participants who can, but don't have to,
cause problems in a group. I suspect all of us bear these
tendencies to some degree. Lest readers get nervous, I confess to
finding myself listed among them at times. I'm not trying to stifle
individual personalities in favor of "groupthink" and behavior,
but to offer some help in handling extreme cases. When the
welfare of the group is threatened by the behavior of a given
individual, we must act to preserve group interaction and
exchange. The group looks to the facilitator to protect them from
the monopolizers and others. When we do, they love us. When
we don't, they leave.

Chapter 7

Working with Parents in Groups

Like children and adults, groups go through stages of development, each demanding special attention. Five commonly accepted stages are *forming*, *norming*, *storming*, *performing*, and *adjourning*.

Forming

Choosing our subject. The first question in the formation of any group should be, "What subject is the group most interested in?" In other words, why is the group meeting? One of the most common errors in forming a parent education group is being too general in approach and content. "An Evening for Parents" tells us little. Are we going to be discussing toilet training or adolescent peer pressures? The generality of the title is not likely to draw parents for either group. The more specific the offering, the more likely it is to attract participants. Parents whose children are long past toilet training don't want to be bothered with those earlier worries when they're struggling with possible drug and alcohol use. Parents with toilet trainees aren't interested in adolescent pressures, either.

A group, by definition, is a collection of people with a common denominator. Our task in forming the group lies in establishing that denominator. The denominator can be children's age: Tackling the Terrific Twos; Preteens and Peer Pressures; And Then God Created Seven-Year-Olds; Guiding Your Child into the Right College. It can be an emphasis on prevention: Building Good Self-Esteem in Early Childhood; Recognizing Your Family's

Strengths; Making Stress Work for Your Family; Learning to Play Again as a Family. Or it can be based on issues or problems: Single-Parent Families Can Be Healthy; Filling Empty-Nest Spaces; When Parenting Styles Don't Mesh; Where Did All the Money Go?; Creating a Successful Stepfamily.

Experience tells us that parents respond more readily to sessions offering help on issues they are facing at the moment rather than on those ahead of them. So we touch the "what's-in-it-for-me?" nerve by narrowing our topic to hook specific parents. By defining the common denominator, we offer a promise to potential attendees: "This is what we will discuss, and it will be of value to you—not later, but right now in your daily life." When offering prevention-based sessions, we promise parents that if they focus on communication, shared responsibility, and conflict resolution now, they may be saved from greater problems later.

Titling the session. Once we have established our group denominator, we need to pay careful attention to the title of our offering. In the past, the tendency was to reach for negative titles to hook parents: Coping with Teenagers; Surviving Divorce. I've found that parents respond more readily to positive titles. When possible, rework your title to describe specific content in a positive and promising tone. Here are some examples.

Negative	Positive
Overcoming School Phobias	Helping Your Child Like School
Surviving Adolescence	Parents and Those Wonderful Teens
Keeping Kids out of Trouble	Rearing Good Kids
Dare to Discipline	Disciplining with Love
Help! My Kid Is Driving Me Crazy!	Family: A Place Where We Drive Each Other Crazy and Like It

Negative	Positive
Child Development	Childhood: From One Delightful Stage to Another
We Never Have Time Just for Us	Wasting Time Together and Loving It
Handling the Hyperactive Child	Appreciating Your Highly Active Youngster
Overcoming Poor Communication in the Family	Can We Talk? You Bet We Can!

We need to beware of titles that implicate potential attendees. Few of us would offer a session "For Abusive Parents," but I once ran into a pastor who told me he had no troubled marriages in his congregation. "Really?" I responded. "How do you know?" He replied, "I offered an evening for those in troubled marriages and nobody came." He was both perpetrator and victim of an implicating title.

Even the questions we ask to attract attention to a workshop can be insulting. A marvelous, horrible example of an implicating brochure is:

Do you ever have problems with your children because you:

    ____ get drunk?

    ____ get mad at your spouse and take it out on the kids?

    ____ are immature yourself?

    ____ are ignorant of the way children develop?

Some parents are even put off by the term "parent education," because they view it as remedial rather than preventive and fear that attendance implies failure. Positive titles like "Making Good Families Better" help offset this fear.

Describing the session. Once we've established our title, we turn to the description or blurb detailing content and particulars—date, location, cost, and time. In addition to offering information, the blurb should attempt to hook parents into attending. I find the "3-W" hook—wonder, worry, wish—to be one effective way of tempting parents. It can be edited to fit most topics. Here are examples from three workshops I've offered to different groups:

Reclaiming the Family Calendar

Parents: Do you . . .

- wonder if your family life is too busy?
- worry that time is slipping by too quickly?
- wish you had more skills in prioritizing?

All parents have these feelings at times. We invite you to join other parents and parent educator Dolores Curran to share frustrations and solutions in unraveling an overscheduled family calendar.

> Date: January 10
> Place: Whitman Elementary School
> 3rd and Broadway
> Time: 7:30-9:30 p.m.
> Cost: Donation

Nurturing Your Family's Faith

Parents: Do you . . .

- wonder if you're really passing on faith in your family?
- worry that your children seem so uninterested?
- wish you had some new ideas on fostering family spirituality?

All parents have these feelings at times. . . .

Working with Parents

Staffs: Do you . . .

- wonder why parents seem so uncooperative at times?
- worry that you aren't meeting family needs?
- wish you had better skills in working with parents?

All professionals have these feelings at times. . . .

Of course, there are many techniques other than the "3-W," which may be overused once we discover the handiness of it. My point is not the catchiness of the description as much as the hook it offers. Here is another I have used with success in staff training publicity:

Working with Parents

Have you ever thrown a parents' meeting and nobody came?

Or they came once but didn't return?

Do your parents sit mutely when you try to get a discussion going?

Do you attract one father for every ten mothers?

Do you always seem to attract the parents who don't need help?

*Have you given up on parents? If so, you
have lots of company.*

We experience these frustrations because we don't know how to work with parents.

Working with Parents is a day designed for teachers, social workers, nurses, religious educators, parenting specialists, voluntary organization leaders—all professionals and volunteers who count parents as a vital part of their work.

Topics include: how to recruit parents, keep them coming back, understand them, enlist them as supporters, and help them focus on their strengths to deal with normal family stresses.

Techniques include: lecture, discussion, role playing, problem solving, technique sharing, and humor.

Dolores Curran has taught parent education at many conferences and universities. In addition, she has directed parenting courses and seminars for fifteen years and is the author of *Traits of a Healthy Family* and *Stress and the Healthy Family*. Her weekly column, "Talks with Parents," reaches four million readers nationally. She is married to a professional educator, is the mother of three, and lives in Colorado.

An effective publicity hook used by David Lamarre-Vincent of New Hampshire to promote a workshop called "Nurturing Children in Peace and Justice" began like this:

"Feel pressured by a lack of time to integrate work, family, and faith? Concerned about raising children in a society filled with injustice and exploitation? Want the support and challenge of meeting with other beleaguered parents?

Come, share your experience. Hear practical suggestions for living simpler lives and experiencing the wholeness of Christian living. Learn how others imaginatively integrate family life, prayer, and social concern."

I strongly encourage staffs to spend considerable effort on the blurb, focusing on these questions:

1. Does the blurb hook the parents we're seeking?
2. Is it inclusive of all kinds of parents, or does it imply "approved" parents only? (I often add to my blurb, "For all kinds of parents: dual, single, step, grand, non, and those in between.")
3. Is there any language ("disadvantaged," "low-income," "hurting") that might offend parents?
4. Does it promise practical help?
5. Does it give parents permission to have problems?
6. Is it positive in tone?
7. Does it clearly indicate proposed content?
8. Is information on setting, date, time, and cost complete and easy to read? Are directions for finding the facility clear? What about parking instructions? Entrance to be used? Is it clear whether this is one session or an ongoing series?

Publicizing the session. Even though I put great importance on title and description, their value is minimal if information isn't disseminated effectively. Once we have title, description, and particulars, this information can be used for brochures, bulletin board notices, posters, press releases, radio spots, and letters sent home with children.

Sometimes we depend too heavily on one publicity vehicle (such as newspapers) rather than the variety available to us. The more vehicles we use, the greater our potential drawing power. People who don't read the paper may read supermarket bulletin boards. A stack of flyers is more effective than a posted notice because people will pick up a flyer, pocket it, and look at it later, whereas they tend to forget poster information. Flyers can be mimeographed or printed cheaply and placed by volunteers in public places and waiting rooms.

Other good locations are libraries, church racks, family counseling centers, YMCAs, child care centers, community and recreation centers, clinic and hospital waiting rooms, schools, beauty shops, fabric and needlework stores, supermarkets, banks, and pediatricians' offices. A short, well-written press release with complete details can be sent to local papers, radio and television stations, La Leche Leagues, Lamaze groups, school and organization newsletters, Montessori schools, church bulletins, community calendars, and parenting publications. Notices can be posted on bulletin boards in supermarkets, churches, schools, shops, libraries, clinics, community centers, spas, and recreation centers.

Two particularly effective communication vehicles are letters sent home with children and word-of-mouth. The word-of-mouth approach is the best publicity device, but it requires priming. Most institutions and organizations have a core group of active parents who are happy to set up sports leagues, field days, Halloween parties, and the like. If we invite these parents to have coffee with us, explain the session we're offering, and ask their help in getting the word out, they may take some ownership in getting people to attend.

Once, when working with a school staff to set up a parenting session, I discovered that the person in charge of publicity had sent one notice to the local newspaper, and that was all. The attendance situation looked bleak, so I suggested the staff call in ten of their "go-getter" parents for help. Sensing the urgent nature of the problem—we had only four days to publicize and recruit—they took on the challenge with a zest, calling parents, setting up car pools and child care. We ended up with a full house. Even when advance publicity is thorough, it is invaluable to have a core group willing to call and remind parents as the session approaches.

Providing child care. Child care is another area to consider when offering any kind of parenting course or session. It is essential for daytime offerings and important for evenings too if we hope to attract both parents. I worked in Australia and Ireland at a time when child care was largely nonexistent, and I noticed a vast difference in attendance when child care was not offered. We drew few fathers in these two countries because it was assumed that they would stay home to mind the children while the mothers learned better ways of parenting.

Offering child care is not that difficult. Churches and schools often ask volunteers to care for the children, although some hire one or two adults—retired teachers, perhaps—to furnish activities for children during the two hours their parents are in class. For this service a nominal charge is added to the ticket price. One hospital wellness center, which runs a series of parenting evenings, rents a family film video for children and includes popcorn as a bonus.

Deciding whether or not to charge. Cost is usually a consideration. Some private schools offer parenting seminars as a part of a child's tuition. Most institutions charge a fee per session. There are various schools of thought on charging for parent education. Some organizations and institutions feel that a charge prevents parents from attending, especially in economically deprived areas, while others believe that more value is placed on an offering when we have to pay for it. Much, of course, depends on budget and expenses.

One church that is deeply committed to prevention-based parent education has a novel technique for dealing with the cost dilemma. The staff sets five annual sessions in advance and prints ticket booklets that are given to parents when they register children for church school. Having a ticket seems to put more value on the offerings, they say. An added bonus to the ticket book method is that the dates, titles, descriptions, time, and place are printed on each ticket, serving as reminders to parents. "Parents tell us they put the tickets on their refrigerators to remind them," the director of parent education told me.

If there is a cost, it should be publicized clearly. I've been invited to facilitate at school and church workshops where parents have come without money. It's an embarrassment that can be avoided. Sometimes sponsoring organizations do not charge but put out a donation box, an alternative to the charge-or-not issue.

Handling breaks. Planning breaks is also part of the forming stage. If the session is a typical two-hour offering, we need to decide whether to have the break in the middle or at the end. Each has its advantages. Breaking midway is usually preferred, but adults can and do sit through a full-length movie, so if the class is interesting and if they're involved, you may decide not to break. Since some parents leave at breaktime to take baby-sitters home, the midway break can be a disadvantage. I've found that breaks are largely a cultural habit, so I usually go with the tradition established in a given locale.

However, the facilitator must be sensitive to the group's needs. I think of the time I spoke at a conference in which I was scheduled from 9:45 a.m. until 12:30 p.m. "When do you want to break?" I asked my hostesses. "We aren't going to break," they said. "But they will need a break," I replied. Nearly three hours and no break planned! I tried to persuade them, but they were adamant. Halfway through, I said to the group of 700, "You're looking uncomfortable. Do you need a break?" "Yes," they replied in unison. We took a break.

I always try to let participants know at the outset when we will break, and I ask someone to volunteer to give me the time-out sign five minutes before break so I can bring that portion of class to a close. Don't be afraid to take your break a little early if the timing seems right. Sometimes we're faced with the situation of beginning a new topic with only five or ten minutes to go until break. Then it's easy to say, "This seems like a good time to break. We'll start up again in fifteen minutes."

Getting people back after a lively break can be troublesome. Often I ask the sponsors to be responsible. If I'm working with a group for the entire day with several breaks, I use a little bell. In working with staffs in Ireland, I found my participants much more relaxed than Americans are about starting and reconvening on time. To my chagrin, I tried to impose an American pace on my first daylong group, instead of going with their tempo. As my tour wore on, I became comfortable with the cultural idea that schedules are to be viewed more as suggestions than as straitjackets.

My Irish participants also gave me a valuable insight. During "tea break," their conversations were ear-splitting. As I wandered around, I heard them discussing the content of the workshop with one another. Their breaks were natural small groups, a kind we probably wouldn't have achieved if we had scheduled them.

In America, we operate differently. We tend to adhere to the printed schedule. When we don't, it makes some participants nervous, even irritable. That's why I try to start on time, even if there's a habit of waiting for latecomers. If we are scheduled to start at 8:00 and we wait until 8:20, we are training people to be late. Worse, we punish those who are on time by making them wait for those who aren't. Even in the United States, different cultures have different concepts of time. If you live and work in an area where the idea of promptness means only a half-hour late, then go with the tradition rather than trying to impose your value system. Simply build lateness into the session. If you want to start at 7:30, announce a 7:00 starting time. I've also noticed that in areas where people are prompt, they tend to depart promptly, while latecomers sometimes hang around after the session. Basically, we have the same amount of time available to us. If we start late, we can also finish late.

Choosing a site. Site and facility also are fundamental in the forming stage. Some parents are intimidated by school settings, especially classrooms. I find church sanctuaries deadly in processing groups, because people are reluctant to talk and laugh in church and the pews are immovable. If I must use a sanctuary, I refuse to use the altar or pulpit. Another problem with sanctuaries as workshop environments is the habit people have of leaving the first several pews empty. A facilitator can feel very lonely up there. Instead, I stand at the top of the aisle to have better physical contact with people, and I walk down the aisle frequently to elicit response from those in the rear pews.

Once I was invited to teach a session on family strengths in a Los Angeles church, and everything went wrong. The first six pews were vacant. In order for parents to see the flip chart, it had to be on the altar. Nobody would talk or laugh. It was ghastly and I quickly switched to a lecture format, assuming from the lack of responsiveness that there was little interest in the process.

But when we took our break and went to a well-lighted and pleasant community room in the basement, everyone came to life. They made the remarks and asked the questions they hadn't asked upstairs. On the spot, I went to the adult educator in charge and asked to resume in the basement. She wasn't happy about it, although she acceded to my request. The second half of the evening was a totally different experience. When I asked the educator why she had set up the session in the sanctuary rather than the church hall, she replied, "Because it's so much prettier there."

Don't be afraid to assert yourself when choosing a facility or rearranging a room for maximum participation. Even if your local mental health center has a lovely conference room, avoid the center like the plague. Parents won't attend preventive education at a center known for treating disorders. One study on parent education found that participants prefer a church locale to a school, hospital, or mental health facility. Community centers, libraries, and recreation centers are preferred next, because they are nonthreatening.

If you do use a church, try to get several churches to sponsor the event so that parents will realize you are simply using a church building rather than endorsing a doctrinal approach to parenting. Many churches that would like to offer parenting courses but don't have the resources are willing to offer their space to outside groups.

The Extension Service Home Economics Program, part of the State Department of Agriculture, has been in the forefront of parent education, but it has no facilities of its own. "We use library and bank community rooms, churches, schools—whatever we can get—deliberately," a county extension director told me. "We don't want a conference building of our own because we want to go to the people, rather than have them come to us."

I teach many parent education sessions at nearby retreat centers. Most denominations have one that is designed for classes and meetings as well as for relaxation. Some schools, churches, and community centers are setting up family resource centers, with rooms dedicated to books, videos, toys, and other materials useful to parents. These are often unused classrooms transformed into comfortable living rooms where parents can meet, browse, wait for children, and hold small-group meetings.

I urge you to consider establishing such a center. It is a wonderful location for holding ongoing, small parenting classes. Its very existence says, "Parents and family are an important part of our mission." For information on how one school developed a resource center, read "Establishing a Parent Education Resource

Center" by Patricia Edmister in *Changing Family Lifestyles.* (See Resources.)

Location and transportation are factors in choosing a site. Is it convenient for people to reach? If a significant number of potential attendees don't drive, is it on the bus line? Is it in a safe part of town? If not, can you offer escorts to the parking lot and bus stop? Is the school or building identified on the outside, or will parents unfamiliar with the area be faced with several possible buildings from which to choose—in the dark? If it's a building with several entrances, will there be lights and signs indicating which door to use? Will this information be on your publicity flyer? I once taught a seminar in a labyrinth of a building at a local college where all sorts of night classes were being conducted. I discovered later that several parents searched futilely for our room; eventually, they gave up and went home.

Arranging the room. Once you decide on the facility, consider the room arrangement. Can you use semicircles or U-shapes rather than straight rows to ensure better group eye contact? If it's a long, rectangular room in which participants sitting in the back will have to strain to see, can you turn the chairs a half-turn and use the room horizontally?

I find some hosts to be unaware of alternative seating arrangements, which is the first factor I consider when I enter a room. Sometimes we have to be more assertive than we like when a room or schedule has been carefully set up but is all wrong for our purposes.

If we're processing, we want as much face-to-face contact among participants as possible. If the blackboard is on the wrong wall, don't sacrifice effective seating to use it. Ask for a flip chart instead. If there's one door in the front of the room, classroom style, turn the chairs around so the door is in the back and latecomers won't distract the group.

My favorite setting is one in which participants are able to sit at tables. They can take notes more easily, rest their elbows, and have a place to put coffee cups and handouts. If I have a large room with a small number of participants, I remove excess chairs, forcing parents to sit closer to the front in a semicircle. It's difficult to bond a group if it scatters itself with empty spaces between participants.

Using transparencies. Many presenters use overhead projectors effectively, but, alas, others do not. Familiar errors include using too many transparencies or transparencies with small print, throwing them up too fast and removing them before participants have had a chance to read them, standing in front of the projector so that half the transparency is blocked, placing them crookedly so viewers have to cock their heads to read them, moving them around jerkily so they correspond with the speaker's words, and leaving one on during the entire presentation, which distracts listeners from further content. When overheads are misused in these ways, viewers simply give up trying to see them or to connect their content with the verbal content of the facilitator.

I overheard a number of graduate students mocking a professor who was addicted to overhead transparencies. Whenever the class asked a question, he replied with, "I've got a transparency here somewhere . . ." and proceeded to search through voluminous piles for it instead of simply answering the question. One day, one of the students said, "I don't want a transparency on this, but what is the rationale behind . . ." and proceeded with his question. The class tittered, but the professor missed the point. "It's a difficult question to answer without the overhead," he replied, searching through his pile. Eventually, the class stopped asking questions.

Offering books and materials. A word here on selling or loaning books and materials to participants. Determine where the tables for coffee and book displays will be placed. Will they impede movement during breaks? Will they serve as bottlenecks? Will they be too out-of-the-way for parents to browse?

Parent educators find that parents will buy or borrow books on parenting if they are available at the session, but they rarely make a trip to the bookstore or library to obtain them. If we want maximum effectiveness and follow-up in our training efforts, it's worthwhile having books, tapes, and videos for purchase or loan. If there's a bookstore in town, invite the owner to bring pertinent books and to staff a sales table. If not, ask the local librarian if a staff member can bring books and loan them out to be returned to the library later. Sometimes I bring my personal library, and the hosts take orders after parents have examined the books.

If you or other facilitators are published authors, bring personally autographed books, although this may be difficult if you're traveling by air. Many sponsors aren't aware that some publishers offer a discount on their author's books where the author is speaking. The sponsoring group can help offset expenses in this way. Once, when I spoke at a large conference, the sponsors actually made a profit, because they ordered and sold enough books to more than offset my stipend and expenses. Publishers usually ask sponsors to pay shipping costs, but they accept unsold returned books without penalty.

I like to have free materials on the table as well, perhaps newsletters and information from other parenting groups. Sometimes I ask sponsors to obtain permission to photocopy a magazine article pertinent to my topic and have it available to participants. Anything we can do to extend the follow-up is good educational procedure.

Compiling a mailing list. If the session is open to the general public and parents attend from a variety of geographical areas, it's useful to have a sign-up sheet for names and addresses so participants can be informed of subsequent sessions. Since people are wary of signing anything, suspecting that they might be visited by salespeople the next day, it's helpful to say, "We're passing around a sign-up sheet. If you want to be informed of future offerings, put your name and address on it, and we'll let you know."

One group used a clever approach to obtain a mailing list. They asked participants to put their names and addresses on the back of their tickets or on a slip of paper for a drawing for a copy of my book *Stress and the Healthy Family.* This gave them a mailing list of nearly 200 parents. The idea of a drawing for a free book, course, or membership adds a bit of spice to the session and helps bond the group. I frequently donate one of my books for this purpose when I am the speaker.

Planning refreshments and allowing for handwork. Refreshments deserve some mention here. Coffee and cookies are the usual offering, but many do not like to drink coffee at night, so I like the practice of offering a cold drink—punch, lemonade, or iced tea—in addition to a hot drink. Sometimes an urn of hot water, tea bags, and instant coffee are put out, but this slows down the line considerably. If there's a large group, some members don't get their drink until the end of the break.

A group in western Canada puts out a tray of apples and cookies. Because of a changing attitude toward sugar and sweets, some groups offer popcorn, which participants seem to like very much. A group in Hawaii offers trays of fruit.

If the conference session is to last a full day, I find that coffee and doughnuts in the morning and cold drinks and popcorn in the afternoon are ideal. Some morning groups like to offer coffee before the first session, and this does seem to relax participants. However, to avoid delaying starting time, be sure you make it clear that coffee time is scheduled thirty minutes before the session begins.

I don't mind when people bring their coffee into class or get up for a refill during the session, but some facilitators do, and some sponsors do not want refreshments in the conference room. It's best to check out expectations beforehand. Nor do I mind participants bringing handwork such as knitting to the group, especially if it is a support group that meets regularly. Some people concentrate better if their hands are busy. I sometimes add to my flyer, "Bring your handwork if you like." This invitation tells potential attendees that the environment is likely to be relaxed and homey, rather than rigid and academic.

One of my most effective sessions was titled, "Parenting—Handwork and Heartwork." It was a morning workshop for mothers only. We began by having each woman show her needlework. Then, as they settled into their work, I processed them on effective rule- and consequence-setting with children. They were unusually responsive. I suggest the idea to readers who work with women-only groups. On our flyer we added, "Women without handwork are welcome, too. Some of us learn better if our hands are busy, others don't."

Providing for participants' comfort. Smoking? No longer. It raises intense anger in groups. But do furnish a place for smokers during the break, even if it's outside. When I facilitated a full-morning session with first sergeants in Korea, most of them smoked, so we called a five-minute break every forty-five minutes, rather than a fifteen-minute midway break.

A final nuts-and-bolts consideration in the forming stage is that of temperature and ventilation. I am sometimes astonished at how little attention is paid to this. If people are shivering with cold or fanning themselves in the heat, they are not able to concentrate on what's being said. If you find yourself in a facility with either of these conditions, look for alternatives. Don't be afraid to say, "Let's move to the cafeteria or library."

Once I was scheduled to teach a daylong session for parent educators at a college. The air conditioning in the building failed. There were no windows in our room and by late morning the heat had become unbearable. I sent a volunteer to scout alternatives, and we ended up in a corner of the student lounge. We had to deal with distractions, but it was preferable to the heat. If we hadn't moved there, we would have gone outside or canceled.

Watch for stuffiness in the room. Open windows and doors if people start yawning or taking on glazed expressions. If there's little you can do about ventilation, give the group several short breaks instead of one longer one.

Uncomfortable chairs can be the bane of facilitators, but there's little you can do about them other than empathize and take frequent stretch breaks. When faced with this dilemma, I invite attendees to stand against the wall or sit on the floor if they begin to feel uncomfortable. When the whole group begins shifting, it's time to take a stretch break—maybe even lead them in a few aerobic stretches. One skilled presenter has the group stretch their arms to the ceiling, then out in front, to the side, and to the back. They conclude with a massage to their posteriors. It brings both laughter and relief to the group.

Of all the housekeeping problems that arise, the most frequent is inadequate sound. If people have to strain to hear, if there's a screech or echo in the sound system, or if outside noise prevents hearing, the best process and content in the world are useless. I recall the time a group of churches offered a full-day conference on parenting, drawing over 400 parents. There were many speakers and a great amount of money was spent on publicity, travel, and stipends. The conference was held in a gymnasium. The loudspeakers faced into the balconies where fans sat during games. But the conference seats were on the floor of the gym. The sound flew to the balconies and reverberated throughout the huge gym. Nothing could be done because the sound engineer wasn't available, and nobody else had the expertise or permission to correct the problem. It was incredible to the speakers and parents alike that the planning staff had not checked out the sound system in advance. Expecting speakers and listeners to compensate for an inadequate sound system is folly. The whole day was a waste of money and effort.

Encouraging group cohesion. Once we have considered the housekeeping details for a group, we are faced with forming individuals into a group. I've already discussed some techniques for achieving bonding, and, of course, the empowerment process itself is conducive to quick connecting. The most familiar method of forming people into a group is self-introductions. If you use this method, I suggest adding a question to help members remember one another. I may say, "Will you tell us your name, and the number and ages of your children? Also, tell us what you enjoy doing in your spare time, if you're lucky enough to have any." Their responses help others remember names by associating unique details to individuals.

We need to pay particular attention to those who come alone and to those who appear timid and uncomfortable. One popular facilitator keeps an empty file folder open on his lectern, making notes as people introduce themselves. During the session, he will direct comments to individuals: "When you're doing your cross-word puzzle, maybe you could ask your son for help," or "With four boys, I'll bet you get a lot of conversation about cars at the dinner table." Parents really respond to him because he remembers them and what they said.

All the above areas are factors to consider in the forming stage of group interaction. Paying careful attention to this stage is important, because it lays the foundation for the stages that follow.

Norming

As described in earlier chapters, the norming stage is the period during which we state our goals, expectations, proposed content, and schedule. We also discuss rules at this time. When processing, I often say to a new group, "I hope you will share your wisdom, experiences, and failures with us so that this doesn't turn into a two-hour lecture. But remember, nobody has to talk. Some people learn just by listening."

This is the time to discuss rules such as the ones suggested in Chapter 4: "I won't be afraid to disagree with you, if you aren't afraid to disagree with me"; "Everyone who wants to talk gets to talk once before anyone gets to talk twice"; "We can discuss what was said in here, but we won't identify the speakers."

I have a friend, a highly respected parent educator, who uses the norming stage to discuss a contract between himself and parents. His is a six-week course in family communication. "The contract between us," he tells parents at the opening session, "is that you can count on my being here, and I can count on your being here. As adults, is this a reasonable contract?" They nod. He continues. "If, for some reason, I can't be here, I will call and let you know. I expect the same courtesy from you." He then puts his phone number in large digits on the board and says, "If you can't attend, I expect you to let me know or I will wonder if I'm not hitting the mark with you. Family communication takes commitment, and so does this course. If you can't agree with this contract, perhaps another course would be better for you."

I admire him for his candor. One of the most destructive frustrations the parent educator experiences is haphazard attendance, which means unpredictable class size as well as students who have missed earlier sessions but expect to catch up at the expense of others who have attended faithfully. By making parents aware of his or her expectations early in the course, the facilitator offsets potential problems later.

Storming

Storming is the stage where most groups break down. It occurs when people feel comfortable enough with one another to disagree. Instead of avoiding this stage we should welcome it, because it precedes performing. If we avoid the storming stage, we will not be able to perform or achieve our goals adequately.

If we deal with disagreement and conflict positively and openly, we will move on to performance with ease. Only when people are able to disagree respectfully will they be able to come up with mutually acceptable solutions. Because those of us drawn to the caregiving professions tend to be peacemakers, it's understandable that group conflict may disturb us. I've seen numerous meetings where staffs and boards skirt controversial issues that must be faced if objectives are to be achieved. Familiar reactions to the first sign of conflict are, "Things seem to be getting heated," or "It looks like we aren't agreeing on this, so maybe we better table it for another time."

If we establish from the outset—in the norming stage—that storming is a healthy part of performance, parents and staffs won't fear it when it emerges. When the first parent in a group disagrees with me or with another parent, I say, "Wonderful. We've reached the point where we feel free to disagree. Now we can get on with sharing what works and what doesn't."

As valuable as storming is in a group, it can be destructive if it causes hurt feelings or if people feel put down. To avoid destructive conflict, the facilitator needs to move from discussing the person to discussing the issue. If a conflict arises over whether "good" mothers work outside the home, for example, angry feelings can erupt on both sides and damage group rapport. Before these feelings are allowed to emerge, the facilitator takes control, saying, "Let's look at the positives and negatives of working and parenting simultaneously. What are the positives?" We are staying with the topic, but not allowing it to become an emotional or moral issue.

Sometimes I use the first disagreement to stop and discuss conflict resolution in the staff or family. It's a good place for a mini-lecture. I discuss the following five methods (as seen on the handout in Appendix F) and ask the group for advantages and disadvantages of each.

- Avoidance: Sidestepping or clouding an issue, postponing discussion, withdrawing from or denying the conflict.
- Accommodation: Sacrificing one's own concerns to satisfy the concerns of another person, often because one fears hurting the other person's feelings.
- Competition: Pursuing one's own wishes at the expense of the other person.
- Compromise: Each person giving up something in order to resolve the conflict quickly.
- Collaboration: Exposing feelings beneath the conflict and coming up with the solution most satisfactory to all.

Families and staffs with the highest levels of stress tend to use the first three methods, while those with controlled stress reach for compromise and collaboration.

I ask parents to select which method or methods they tend to reach for first when there's conflict in the family. I then use a hypothetical conflict to teach collaboration. Many families do not use collaboration because they don't know how. One of the greatest skills we can give families is the art of compromise and collaboration. I find that parents are immensely interested in learning better ways of dealing with family conflict, but they don't know where to go to learn how to do this. (For more information on conflict resolution in the family, see my book *Stress and the Healthy Family*.)

Performing

If we've prepared the first three stages well, our goal of effective parent education will follow. Performance simply means achieving the goals we have set. As discussed in earlier chapters, listening to needs, processing solutions, and offering content on effective parenting skills all emerge in the performance stage.

Adjourning

This final stage sums up the group's effort. Sometimes groups adjourn without having addressed the content or getting to the performance stage, a situation sure to diminish the attraction of further parent education offerings.

Evaluation is a part of the adjourning stage and plays an essential role in future effectiveness. It also gives participants an opportunity to voice disappointments and praise. Sometime during the latter part of a seminar or in the last session of a series, we can give parents a simple evaluation form to complete so that we can learn what was most and least valuable to them.

I pay great attention to parents' evaluations and use them to improve future workshops. If several participants say that they would have liked more time spent on helping children deal with anger, I make a note to myself to extend this mini-lecture next session. If they indicate physical discomforts, I try to avoid those in the future. Additional information of value to planners and speakers includes where people heard about the seminar, what topics they would like addressed in the future, and what they would change to make sessions more effective.

Some planners and parent educators find it painful to read evaluations because they take suggestions as personal criticisms, rather than resources for improvement. This is a great error. Even those most pleased with a workshop have suggestions to offer that may improve future classes. We need to accept that we are only likely to please 80 percent of any given group. I've found this borne out in my experience. Most evaluations may be marked excellent in a group, but two or three respondents mark every category as poor. A seminar isn't likely to be excellent and poor simultaneously.

If the majority of the evaluations are positive, we can assume the few disappointed attendees were seeking something other than the content promised, or perhaps personal therapy rather than preventive education. Perhaps they felt forced to attend, and completing an evaluation negatively is their only way of venting their resentment. I'm not implying that we should ignore negative evaluations or consider them the work of cranks, but that we judge evaluations as a whole rather than with our all-too-human tendency to focus on the 20 percent that may be critical.

I like to read the evaluations entirely and then write a summary of the major points. Here's one of my recent summaries:

Liked: participation; handouts; pace; information on teen development.

Would have changed: lengthy opening introductions (thanking people, etc.); outside noise.

Heard about session: most from letters sent home with kids; a few from newspaper and radio.

Want in future: more on teens and preteens, especially peer pressures; more on young adults living at home; dealing with too many kids' activities, especially sports; money management; parenting together rather than separately.

Another part of adjourning occurs when people ask to continue, especially if the course has been ongoing and the group has bonded. I believe it is a mistake to continue beyond the stated number of sessions, even if some parents request it. Others who committed themselves to three or six sessions may not want to continue, but feel pressured to either do so or be left out.

If parents ask to continue, we can offer another session or series in a few weeks or, better still, encourage them to continue on their own with a little help from us. Since a major part of our role is to develop parent support groups, we can encourage continuance, not dependency. But we can help leaders who have emerged from the group by offering ideas and generally making ourselves available for questions and advice. I've seen several parent support groups form after a series of sessions. Others would like to continue, but find it difficult without support.

Finally, adjourning means summing up what we learned, discussing how to follow it up, and saying goodbye to one another. It puts closure on the group and, we hope, gives all of us a sense of achievement.

In concluding this chapter, I reemphasize that each stage in the development of the group—forming, norming, storming, performing, and adjourning—is fundamental to achieving effective results. When we neglect one stage, it affects the others. When we put effort into each stage, the final product, like a well-balanced child, projects a sense of wholeness.

Chapter *8*

Working with Parents Individually

Although most of the material presented thus far involves working with parents in groups, there are times when it is necessary to meet with one or two parents individually. These may be routinely scheduled parent conferences or meetings specifically requested by either the parent or the professional to discuss a child's needs or behavior. Much excellent material has been written on how to conduct effective teacher-parent and social worker-parent conferences, and many of the techniques we've discussed for working with groups can be used with individuals. However, individual conferences require some specific techniques as well. Whether conferences are routine or requested, the following feelings and reactions need to be understood and addressed.

1. We can assume that parents will be anxious, and perhaps defensive. Even in routine conferences, there is parental fear. Most of us do not have perfect children and, when an imperfection is pointed out to us, we're likely to become defensive. We perceive any mention of our children's problems as criticism of our parenting. The exception to this are parents who always hear wonderful things about their children.

A personal example will illustrate this defensive reaction. One of our children was a self-imposed perfectionist to whom an A was not enough. This child needed to earn the top A or would feel like a failure. We recognized this need and tried to reduce the self-pressure. We were eventually successful, but for years at parent conferences we heard polite suggestions that we reduce pressure on this child. We became defensive, insisting that the pressure was self-imposed and that we were doing everything we could to diminish it. Teachers' reactions were skeptical, which increased our frustration. If teachers had empathized with us and suggested practical ways of diminishing the self-imposed pressure on this child, we would have been grateful instead of angry.

Often parents deny a problem or insist that it is the school's, coach's, or clinic's fault. This is their way of reacting to what they assume is criticism of themselves. Teachers and other professionals go crazy inside when parents say, "He doesn't do that at home," or "She wasn't like that until she joined this league." If professionals anticipate this reaction and learn to deal with defensiveness and denial objectively, we will be able to enlist parents as cooperators rather than rivals. How do we accomplish this?

2. We can assume that any problem we experience with the child is a problem parents experience at home. Children who lie at school are likely to lie at home. Poor losers on the playing field are likely to be poor losers in the backyard. Kids who fight medical care in the clinic fight it even more tenaciously at home. Preteens who scoff at religious rituals in class are better scoffers during prayer time at home.

When professionals comment on any of these behaviors to parents, we are giving words to a behavior they've already experienced and have not been able to deal with effectively. It's only natural that they react defensively, perhaps even with denial, because what they hear us saying is, "Your child has this problem, and you don't care enough about it to deal with it." This isn't true, of course. We don't mean to imply parental neglect, but that's how parents perceive our words. They're likely to become resentful and uncooperative, maybe even openly angry, and the conference may break down with anger on both sides.

I've seen this happen many times, and I have experienced it myself. Conferences turn into a contest of wills and words between parents and professionals. How do we avoid this trap and enlist parents in the mutual objective of dealing with unwanted behaviors in children?

3. We acknowledge the problem with empathy and offer parents skills in dealing with it. Empathy and counseling skills are our most valuable gifts to parents. We want to get them on our side as quickly as possible. Instead of saying, "We're having a problem with Mark's tendency to fib," we say, "At this age, kids often lie rather than face the consequences of what they do. I'll bet this drives you crazy at times." Instead of saying, "Tom is a poor loser, and we can't let him play unless he shapes up," we say, "Losing is tough on nine-year-olds. You probably already know that. Maybe I can help with some ideas we use at the YMCA to help kids learn to lose." Instead of saying, "She's going to have to settle down and take this medicine," we can say, "A typical four-year-old, isn't she? Okay, here are some tricks we use to get kids to take their medication."

In these situations and others like them we are acknowledging the problem, stating its normality, empathizing with parents, and offering counseling skills. When we do this, we have parents in our corner. We have become allies instead of opponents. Parents, when they feel empathy from us, usually experience immense relief. They feel understood. They are no longer alone in dealing with the problem because they've been offered professional help in a compassionate way. Some will begin admitting to the scope of the problem: "Yes, his lying drives us crazy. We've tried everything—spanking, no television, grounding—but nothing works. We don't know what else to do."

Some may break into tears. Hand them a tissue and say, "You're not the first parent in here who has had this problem. Let's go through some ideas of what you might try. Why do you think he lies?" The parent's head shakes sorrowfully. "I don't know."

"Could you try this? The next time he lies, instead of getting angry, look at him sadly and say, 'Mark, I'm getting worried about you. You're getting into such a habit of lying that none of us can believe anything you say anymore. I'd like to make a deal with you. The next time you're tempted to tell a lie and don't, tell me. Just say something like, "I could have lied, but I didn't." If you do that, I promise I won't get mad.'"

"But," the parent might object, "how do I punish him for what he's done? Won't he misbehave even more if he knows I'm not going to get mad?" (Be prepared for parent skepticism at any new technique offered.)

"He might, but he might not, once he knows you're pleased with him for admitting to what he's done," I respond. "The first time he says, 'Yes, I did hit him, but I didn't lie,' you might say, 'You're growing up, Mark. I'm disappointed you hit him, but you didn't lie about it, and that makes me happy.'

"Then," I continue, "give the child a smile, and say something like, 'Now, why did you hit him?' You see, now you can deal with the hitting issue."

"I don't know," the parent may say skeptically. "Maybe it won't work." "Maybe not," is my response, "but why not try it for a week and then let me know. If it doesn't work, we can try something else. Meanwhile, I'll use the same technique with Mark here at school."

The tone of a conference may determine its success or failure. When parents realize we understand the problems they face, they will frequently go on to mention other problems with which they want help.

Sometimes I use personal examples with them. For instance, parents may ask me, "How do we get our teenager to go to church without a fight?" I sigh and smile. "Oh, I know all about that. It's been a hassle in our family, too." Their relief is visible. If the parent educator also has had this problem, then perhaps they aren't such failures as parents after all. I continue. "With one of ours, we got so tired of arguing every week that we said, 'We won't argue about your going out on Saturday night, if you don't argue about going to church on Sunday. Is it a deal?' Since he likes to go to a game or a movie on Saturday night, it worked. But he tested us on it, so be ready for that. When he gave us the first argument on Sunday, we said, 'You broke our deal, so you'd better not make plans for next Saturday night.' It only happened once."

Rehashing the same issue is a high cause of stress in family life. That's why we want to help parents put a problem or issue to rest effectively. We can't presume that parents have the skills we've developed for use in the classroom, clinic, or sports league. We need to share these skills with parents who haven't had our opportunity to practice on other people's children.

Both my husband and I were high school teachers in our earlier careers, so we had on-the-job training with teens—learning what works and what doesn't—just to survive in the classroom. The high school teacher learns quickly that humiliating a teen, especially in front of peers, exacerbates any problem. We found that talking with a teen alone and expressing disappointment rather than anger is more effective. We learned that, above all, adolescents treasure fairness. If they say, "I don't think that's fair," and we retort, "Life isn't always fair," we can be sure of either a battle or sullenness. We learned that when they charge us with unfairness, we need to listen to why they think it's unfair and state our reasons for acting in a given manner. They may not accept our reasons, but we will understand each other better and they will appreciate being heard. Sometimes, after listening to them, we realize we are being unfair, but our course of action is the only one open to us. So we acknowledge the unfairness: "Yes, it is unfair that she gets the car again tonight, but the other car is not reliable and she has to get home from work after dark. We'll do the same if it happens to you."

Because my husband and I learned these skills with adolescent students, we were able to use them with our own children when they reached adolescence. But most parents don't have the chance to practice on other people's children. Part of our task as professionals, then, lies in imparting these skills to parents, either in a group setting or individually at conferences. Parents will be grateful if we share what we've learned, and our experiences may give them greater confidence in themselves.

4. *In working with parents, our goal is two-fold: to nurture the child's appropriate behavior and values in our milieu and to help parents instill them at home.* In the past we have generally focused on getting parents to help us, rather than the reverse. Our conference suggestions may have changed a child's behavior in the classroom, but it may have increased stress at home. Any child can be made to behave if parental threats are fearful enough.

I remember a case several years ago where a child was caught stealing from other children's lunchboxes. The teacher called the parents in and talked with them. The child was absent the following two days, and when he returned he was badly bruised. As it turned out, the father had gone directly home after the conference and brutally beaten the boy, who was removed from the home by authorities as a result.

The teacher became so emotionally upset she had to take time off. I'm not implying that the beating was her fault or that she should have ignored the theft. I recount this story only to indicate that a child's school, church, or playtime behavior can be changed dramatically by parents, but sometimes by unhealthy means. Getting the behavior stopped in our environment isn't our only responsibility. Helping parents use positive techniques to modify behavior both at home and in our setting is our goal. When we have an out-of-control child in our setting, we can assume the child is out of control at home. For parent educators, the question, "How can I help the parent get better control at home?" precedes, "How can I get parents to control this child in my setting?"

5. *We must learn to deal with parents' anger.* In a staff session on working with parents, a school social worker asked,

"How do you deal with the angry parent who won't listen to reason?" She went on to explain that she teaches emotionally disturbed children in a public school and that parents of these children often lash out in anger at teachers, at the behavior of other children, and at society in general.

"Why are these parents so angry?" I asked. Another social worker in the group replied quietly, "They're angry at having a handicapped child, and they direct their anger at us. Any problem can be an outlet for them to vent their anger." Nods and comments from the rest in the group affirmed her response.

Parents of children with special needs or ongoing problems may be living with barely contained anger, grief, and guilt. When they see normal, healthy children at play, they feel a sadness that their child will never be able to participate in normal activities. When these favored children ignore or taunt their handicapped children, sadness turns into rage. Who is likely to inherit the fruits of the rage? The teacher, social worker, principal, physician, or other professional in charge.

As parent educators, we can use some guidelines to help us deal with unreasonable parent anger:

- We can realize we are the recipients rather than the instigators of the anger.
- We can empathize by saying to the accusing parent, "I don't blame you for feeling angry. I'd feel angry, too."
- We can indicate to the parent that we know we are being scapegoated: "I don't blame you for feeling angry. In fact, I'm feeling angry for the same reason you are—I'm being made responsible for other people's behavior toward your child. I can't prevent that any more than you can."
- We can refuse, overtly or covertly, to confer if anger is going to block discussion. Refusing overtly, we can say, "We're both too angry to talk about this now. What time can we meet tomorrow when we've both cooled off?" Refusing covertly, we can say, "I'm sorry, but I have to monitor the playground now. When can we meet later this week?"

It's counterproductive to meet with out-of-control, angry parents, because too many words may be spoken that will interfere with our future relationship. A school administrator I deeply admire told me that he refuses to talk with verbally abusive parents, just as he refused to talk with verbally abusive teenagers when he was a high school principal. "There's nothing to be gained," he emphasized. "Treating each other badly is not what we're about."

He told me of an instance when a parent became angry with a child's teacher over some misunderstanding and confronted the teacher in front of the class. When the teacher responded that she couldn't discuss it then, the parent strode angrily to the principal, who listened to her outburst and said, "I'll look into it and call you." Dissatisfied with the lack of immediate action, the parent drove to the administrative headquarters and burst into my friend's office. By now the parent's anger was so intense she was almost incoherent. She burst out with a volley of four-letter words and piled-up, past resentments. Her anger had shifted from the original problem to the runaround she felt she was getting.

My friend stopped her in mid-tirade with, "I'm worried about you. I will get to the root of this, but I can't until you calm down. Come with me to a conference room. I'll get you some coffee, and when you feel under control, come back, and we'll talk about it. We want to give you help, not the runaround." His tone was kind but firm as he led her from the office. Sputtering, she said, "I don't want your ____ coffee. I want action." "Fine," the administrator responded. "You'll get it after we talk. But we can't solve anything with anger, so we'll find you a quiet place so you can get settled." (At times like this it is good to remember that parents who don't care about their children don't get angry with us.)

When dealing with parent anger, we need to dispel the idea that we are giving parents the runaround. Normally that is the first thing they suspect. Parent anger accelerates when we hide behind policy statements: "I'm sorry, but that's school policy," or "I can't do anything about it because of state regulations." Social workers and military family support staff, who are stymied by a plethora of regulations, often feel more frustrated than their angry clients when they are faced with a policy that interferes with aid. Even if they are unable to offer actual support because of regulations, professionals can say, "These regulations are the pits. Let's see if there's any way we can get around them." That statement tells the parent that the professional cares, and it softens the parent's anger.

When our daughter played high school basketball, there was a policy that anyone who missed a week of practice would be benched for the next month's games. We received word that her grandmother was dying and rushed the family to her home a thousand miles away. When we returned after the funeral we sent a note to the coach explaining the situation. He said to our daughter, "Sorry. Policy is policy." And he refused to let her play.

Even though she had practiced faithfully for two months, she was benched the final month of her basketball career because her grandmother had died.

We were furious. We offered to approach a higher school power, but our daughter asked us not to, fearing backlash from the coach. We complied with her feelings, but the whole situation soured us on the coach and the sport. Thus, she was (and we also were) victimized by a bad policy. How do we avoid such a response toward the children and parents we work with?

6. We need to realize that parents serve as advocates for their children. If a child is suffering, who is expected to come to the rescue? Parents, of course. But when they do, they are often labeled troublesome. Few parents want to be troublemakers. They would prefer to remain silent (and many do, although they may vote against us in the next bond election or withdraw their active support) and let the issue resolve itself. When it doesn't, they are forced to step in and protect their children. This parental reaction is as natural as a lioness protecting her cubs. She realizes they are helpless and accepts her responsibility by intervening on their behalf. So it is with parents. When we accept that parents are, by nature, advocates for their children rather than intruders on our turf, we will feel more compassion and less anger toward them.

Ruth Arent, a social worker well known for her work with children and stress, openly informs parents, "You are advocates for your child. Don't be timid about this responsibility. If the teacher has a chart with stars on the bulletin board, and your child comes home feeling lower and lower self-esteem because no matter how hard he tries, he stays at the bottom of the chart, you have a responsibility to step in. As advocate for your child, you need to let the teacher know that every time your child walks in from recess, he gets the message, 'I'm at the bottom.' How long could any of us keep our self-esteem with that kind of visible reminder of our failure?" I suspect all of us have had experience with such charts, visible or otherwise. When parents call attention to these situations, we have two choices: we can either thank them for caring enough to serve as their children's advocates or disparage them for obstructing our efforts.

7. Finally, we can indicate the sincerity of our concern by our positive follow-up. If a parent is troubled and we don't check back to see if the original problem has been resolved satisfactorily, we are missing an excellent opportunity to enlist parental support. When we call or send a note saying, "I haven't heard from you since we talked. Have things improved?" we are telling the parent we care. Even if the parent is not satisfied, our gesture is one of concern and empathy. The parent will feel more positive about us and probably will tell other parents about our interest.

I like the practice many professionals have of sending a positive note home occasionally, something like "Jamie is a great peacemaker on our team," or "Just wanted to let you know how much I enjoy having Sue in Scouts." A popular social worker makes it a point to send a little note annually to each client family with a message of how much she has learned from the family, thanking them for their cooperation. "They hear so many negatives," she said. "A compliment now and then helps." A parent involved in Missouri's "Parents as First Teachers" program summed up its value by saying, "Just to hear I was doing a good job helped." These notes, called "praisegrams" by some, offset the familiar parent experience of hearing from the professionals in their children's lives only when there are problems.

As long as we work with parents, we can expect to face some conflict and anger. We can either resent it and fight it, or anticipate it and make it work for us. In summary, when we are aware of the pitfalls to avoid when working with parents individually and know how to use the techniques suggested in this chapter, we will be able to build more positive, effective partnerships with parents.

Chapter *9*

Parent Education as a Career: Present and Future

I am sometimes startled by teachers, social workers, religious staffs, child care providers, and others who ask me, "How does one get into parent education?" They are already into it by virtue of their work. However, I understand their question. They are asking about the profession of parent education—qualifications, entry, and future.

Because parent education is so new, my answers are likely to be incomplete, but I hope the information provided here will be helpful for those interested in moving from a career that involves parents peripherally to one of working primarily with parents.

Qualifications

One way of entering parent education is through a profession that considers parents a part of its population. Qualifications can vary widely. As in any new profession, many who teach parent education do not hold degrees in it. Nurses, educators, home economists, marriage counselors, members of the clergy, pediatricians, psychologists, social workers, child development specialists, and others, because of their outstanding work with parents, have become prominent in the field of parent education. Many enter unintentionally as a result of offering occasional courses related to parent issues in their own professional areas. I, myself, never intended to get into parent education. I entered through the dual doors of education and adult religious education.

Although you may have a degree in one of the professions mentioned, you may need to fill gaps in your education. A teacher may need courses in family sociology or family dynamics, while a psychologist may need a course in teaching methodology. I suggest you check out the family studies departments of colleges near you. The original state land-grant colleges generally have the most complete range of parent education courses, but some private schools also have excellent programs.

Don't overlook the religious-based colleges. Many offer courses and degrees to a wide ecumenical body. State colleges often offer night and weekend courses, as well as one-day credit seminars on specific topics such as "Working with Parents," "The Family Life Cycle," "Conflict Resolution in the Family," and "Helping Parents Become Sex Educators." The Child Development Center of Metro State College in my home city of Denver, for example, offers eight of these every year.

Students usually are adults who haven't the time to enroll in an ongoing program, people involved in child care, social work, or other service occupations that require specific skills in working with parents. Taking courses is an excellent way to learn new skills and update parenting information for those already in caregiving professions.

If you are interested, call the family studies, early childhood development, education, or social work departments of the colleges near you and ask that your name be placed on mailing lists that will announce offerings in parent education. If your state has a certification process for parent education, check into it by calling your state department of education. If that department isn't in charge of certification, it should be able to refer you to the appropriate department. Some states have placed parent education in the social work or welfare departments, while others have included it in the education or nursing departments.

Individual professionals and institutions such as the Menninger Foundation offer various institutes around the country that can lead to qualification and certification. I find the journal *The Family Therapy Networker* valuable in listing such offerings.* I also recommend joining the Family Resource Coalition for updates on institutes, legislation, and programs around the country. The Center for the Improvement of Child Caring (CICC), in cooperation with the Los Angeles County Office of Education, offers a wide variety of training programs for potential and qualified parent educators who want to stay abreast of new

---

*For the address of this journal and of organizations and institutions that follow, see Resources.

techniques, programs, research, and developments. In addition to training leaders in the most familiar parenting programs, the CICC offers training in specific kinds of parent education, such as "Effective Black Parenting," "Los Niños Bien Educados" for Spanish-speaking parents, programs in nurturing for abusive parents, programs for teenage parents and their children. CICC also offers technical assistance in implementing, marketing, maintaining, and evaluating all parent training programs.

Another option for obtaining certification is through the National Council on Family Relations (NCFR), which might be called the umbrella professional association for the family-related professions. Because the NCFR membership is heavily loaded with psychologists, many of whom work in prevention-based research, much good resource material emanates from the NCFR. The NCFR has implemented a certification process, called the NCFR Family Life Educator Certification, for potential and practicing parent educators. The NCFR is noted for its careful scrutiny of educational background and experience.

Parent education comes under many labels. You may find it identified as a degree in family studies, human development, or family ministry. Make a careful investigation to assure that the program you are considering will actually lead to the degree you are seeking. I have a friend from Ireland who enrolled in a two-year master's course in family ministry, only to discover it was basically a religious studies course. He obtained his degree, but not an education in working with families.

On a national level, certain universities stand out in the family studies field. Pennsylvania State University, the University of Minnesota, Brigham Young University, the University of Wisconsin, Temple University, Cornell University, and the University of Nebraska are familiar to those of us in parent education. But you don't need to limit yourself to these. There are many other fine family studies departments nationwide.

At present, most states do not have minimum standards or certification for parent educators, but this will come. Some states have professional organizations that suggest standards, but these are not officially monitored or enforced. In the final analysis, a background in one of the caregiving professions along with proof of skills in teaching parents effectively seem to be the most widely accepted qualifications.

Entry into the Profession

A second question I'm asked, "Once qualified, how does one enter the field?" is equally difficult to answer. Most of us enter through another profession. It may be as a social worker who decides to give up casework for a parent education position in a community center. I know a child psychologist who so enjoyed teaching parents that he carved a new career for himself by writing and speaking on parenting, offering weekend workshops, and hosting a radio call-in show. "I found I was enjoying prevention work more than therapy," he told me. "It was a little scary at first, becoming self-employed in a relatively new profession, but I've never regretted my move. I love my work."

Most parent educators begin by teaching an occasional evening course while holding another professional position. If and when the invitations to speak and teach become numerous enough, they may give up their full-time work. The decision can be intimidating because it means giving up a steady income for an uncertain one, but I have never known a parent educator who took this career step to return to his or her original profession.

What kind of income can be anticipated as a freelance parent educator? When one first starts out, very little income usually is forthcoming. I often suggest that those who want to establish a name and reputation in the field initially offer their skills without charge to churches and schools. If they are effective, the exposure generates future invitations for which they can charge. I have never done any advertising myself as a parent educator, but every seminar generates one or two invitations.

Most religious and PTA groups pay minimally, perhaps $100 for an evening session. Fees for a popular parent educator, however, can go up to $300 or more for an evening's program and $1,000 or more for a daylong session, especially one requiring travel. Since we set our own fees, each session is negotiable. Some invitations to prestige conferences pay in glory rather than dollars. We must be careful to balance the two.

Some institutions and parent educators use a printed contract that spells out specifics like fees, cancellation monies, and so on. Most of my contracts are verbal, but I ask for a letter of confirmation that states date, time allowance, fee, and expectations. This avoids sticky problems that may arise if one of us doesn't take good notes. State departments of education and social welfare, as well as the military, have complex contracts with sometimes confusing terminology. Don't be afraid to ask, "What does this mean?"

I suggest you develop a personal information sheet or biography that you enclose with your first letter. It can be useful for publicity and book ordering purposes, as well as introductions. In my biography, I use the following categories: Education, Teaching, Commissions, Honors and Awards, Publications, Books, Lectures, and Personal.

I encourage beginning parent educators to initially develop one or two specific areas of expertise, rather than range over the whole field of parent education. "Raising Children with Good Self-Esteem" or "Parent-Teen Communication" are good examples. Few of us are knowledgeable in all areas of parenting. I know one self-employed parent educator who speaks solely on effective discipline, while another talks only about preventing drug and alcohol abuse. Both are in great demand.

Find the area that most appeals to you and develop a workshop presentation around it. Your reputation will grow from it. However, don't get locked into only one niche. Be open to developing new areas of interest. I do so constantly. While I'm best known for my work on family strengths, I range far afield when it interests me. In the past year I have addressed groups on teenage suicide, dual-career marriages, and military family life. However, each new topic takes considerable research and study.

An effective parent educator must keep up with research and trends in family issues and policies. I suggest you develop the habit of reading, or at least skimming, everything you can get your hands on—newsletters, journals, book reviews, and policy statements. I subscribe to at least a dozen family-related journals and magazines and am on the mailing list of another dozen organizations. I have listed several of these in the resource section at the end of this book. When I hear of a new book that might fill a gap in my own education, I examine it at the library. If it is one I want for my personal library, I order it.

Frequently, conferences will select a theme and invite me to address a topic outside my area of specialization. If I feel attracted to the theme and confident of my ability to address it, and if I have the time and desire to develop a presentation in a new area of parent education, I accept. Often, however, I will say, "I don't feel qualified (or comfortable) speaking on that issue." I believe I gain rather than lose credibility by being frank about my competence.

It is helpful for new parent educators to build name recognition by publishing a book or some professional articles, if you have a talent for writing. An occasional article on some family-related issue in a local newspaper or school newsletter also can be valuable, even if there is no payment.

A final suggestion to the beginning parent educator is to develop a simple brochure that describes your area of expertise, lists topic titles, qualifications, and fees, and includes your photo and quotes from parents who have attended your workshops. Distribute these brochures to local churches, community centers, schools, hospital wellness centers, and other institutions that seek program speakers. One new parent educator had phenomenal response from a simple brochure. "People are looking for us," she said to me with surprise.

For those who seek a salaried position in the field of parent education, the most natural places to start are schools, hospitals, churches, and social welfare institutions. Some states are mandating some form of parent education. Every school district in Missouri is now required to offer education to parents as well as children. The state's "Parents as First Teachers" program includes seminars on child development, activities for parents to do at home, and home visits by parent educators. Teachers with a minor in parent education are attractive to school districts today. With the cutbacks in social service budgets during the past few years, many institutions are unable to hire full-time parent specialists. Some school districts will hire a half-time family coordinator. Some parent educators serve two or three churches that have arranged to share salary and expenses.

The most encouraging field today lies in industry. Many businesses, recognizing the link between productivity and family stress, are hiring family specialists to offer courses and to help employees deal with issues at home. I believe we are on the brink of a wide demand for qualified family educators in industry. In my seminars, I meet family education professionals who work for the utility and public service companies, large law firms, and a variety of corporations. These workplaces offer incentives to employees to attend workshops on family-related issues and are constantly seeking facilitators with proven skills. Many facilitators counsel as well as teach. Their role is to help employees learn to better manage money, locate child care services, find support systems, deal with children, prioritize time, manage personal stress, and build self-confidence.

At one time, work problems were allowed to affect the family, but family problems were not allowed to affect work. This attitude is changing dramatically. An employee with a depressed spouse is not as productive as an employee with a happy spouse. A worker with money worries doesn't concentrate as well as one who has learned to manage money. When employees sense that management really cares about their personal family lives, they are more productive, loyal, and satisfied.

Recently I met a retired military chaplain with degrees in marriage and family counseling who is employed by a software producer. He said his company's executive officer told him, "Our employees need help and hope in their personal lives. We figure twenty years of working with military families qualifies you. If you want to offer an optional spiritual dimension for those who want it, like a prayer breakfast or noon Scripture study, fine. Just be a caring person here for our families." He further requested the chaplain to bring to his attention any company policies that might interfere with healthy personal and family life.

Minnesota has taken the lead in developing resources and training in family education within the business community. The Department of Vocational Education offers a series of Work and Family seminars that serve as models for fifteen other states. Seminars offered to businesses by trained family personnel include such topics as management of stress caused by work-family conflicts, effective management of time at home and at work, communication and negotiation within families, assessing family goals and values, decision-making and problem-solving strategies, family roles and responsibilities, handling guilt as a working parent, spending quality time with children, special concerns of single parents, special concerns of dual-employed families, building self-esteem in parents and children, and choosing and using child care.

Industry reaction has been positive. The manager of employee relations at Northwestern Bell said, "Ninety-three percent of the participants rated the quality and content of the presentations as excellent. Employees have expressed gratitude for the opportunity to attend the seminars." Another employer reported, "The feedback has been very positive. The program is consistent with our overall philosophy—we're very people-oriented. We will be looking to the AVTIs (Area Vocational Technical Institutes) as a useful source of training and development."*

---

*For information on the Minnesota Curriculum Services Center, see Resources.

✓ As productivity and loyalty increase in firms that offer special family assistance, others are bound to follow. If you are interested, I suggest contacting a private employment agency that places social workers, psychologists, and other caregivers. It is to these agencies that industry goes. An advertisement in local or national business periodicals is another option. I also encourage you to draft a letter to large corporations and industries in your area, selling them on the value of a family support professional by citing statistics that link productivity and family stress, and offering your qualifications. Some companies see the need but don't take action until someone makes herself or himself available.

If a corporation is interested but doesn't want to budget a full-time salary, consider offering your services on a half-time basis and search for a second part-time employer or for freelance opportunities. Another possibility lies in making your skills available to corporations on a contract basis to conduct certain family-oriented services and courses. Your brochure and a well-written letter are useful in facilitating this approach. Businesses hire similar consultants in sales and technology, and such contracts may open the door to eventual full-time employment. Because managers move frequently from firm to firm, word of your work moves with them.

Let me cite a personal example. I was invited to address a national convention of home economists in Denver on the topic of minimizing work- and family-related stress. From that gathering of 600, I was invited to repeat my presentation at eight state home economist conferences. I accepted three. At one of these three, a vice president of a large chain of discount stores, who sat on the state advisory board for vocational education, invited me to address his managers' yearly conference. At a second, the wife of the president of the state's cattlemen's association invited me to address their annual gathering. At the third, an exhibitor of textbooks and resources inquired about the possibility of my spending a day with the employees of his publishing firm. It was not I, but the topic, that enlisted such interest. None of the three had considered the topic as a possible employee inservice program until they heard about it. Once they did, they became enthusiastic about its relevance to their workplace.

Part of our task, then, lies in educating both the public and businesses on the value of nurturing family well-being. If we don't do it, who will? We know families. We work with parents, and we recognize the high-wire act they perform daily to keep the pieces of the work-family-self puzzle in order.

As advocates of positive and preventive parent education, we are on the threshold of an exciting and worthwhile profession. We can serve families that are heroically trying to retain stability. We can foster healthy values during a time of rapid cultural change. We can assist institutions that are becoming more aware of their responsibility for supporting strong family units.

Although we may define ourselves as educators, coaches, nurses, clergy, psychologists, or social workers, we can add with pride, "And I'm a parent educator."

Resources

Books

Albert, Linda. *Coping with Kids and School: A Guide for Parents.* New York: Ballantine Books, 1985.

Albert, Linda, and Michael Popkin. *Quality Parenting: How to Transform the Everyday Moments We Spend with Our Children into Special, Meaningful Time.* New York: Random House, 1987.

Alvy, Kerby T. *Black Parenting: Strategies for Training.* Studio City, CA: Center for the Improvement of Child Caring, 1987.

_____. *Parent Training: A Social Necessity.* Studio City, CA: Center for the Improvement of Child Caring, 1987.

Alvy, Kerby T., and L. D. Rosen. *Training Parenting Instructors: A National Model for Training Mental Health, Social Service, and Educational Personnel to Deliver Group Parent Training Services in Their Agencies.* Studio City, CA: Center for the Improvement of Child Caring, 1984.

Apgar, Kathryn, et al. *Training Leaders for Family Life Education.* Milwaukee: Family Service Association of America, 1982.

Apgar, Kathryn, and Donald P. Riley. *Life Education in the Workplace: How to Design, Lead, and Market Employee Seminars.* Milwaukee: Family Service Association of America, 1982.

Arent, Ruth P. *Stress and Your Child: A Parent's Guide to Symptoms and Strategies.* Englewood Cliffs, NJ: Prentice-Hall, 1984.

Association for Childhood Education International. *Changing Family Lifestyles: Their Effect on Children.* Washington, DC, 1982.

Auvine, Brian, et al. *A Manual for Group Facilitators.* Madison: Center for Conflict Resolution, 1985.

Baron, Bruce, et al. *What Did You Learn in School Today? A Comprehensive Guide to Getting the Best Possible Education for Your Child.* New York: Warner Books, 1983.

Berends, Polly B. *Whole Child/Whole Parent.* New York: Harper & Row, 1987.

Bettelheim, Bruno, and Anne Freedgood. *A Good Enough Parent: A Book on Child-Rearing.* New York: Random House, 1988.

Bigner, Jerry J. *Parent-Child Relations: An Introduction to Parenting.* New York: Macmillan, 1985.

Brazelton, T. Berry. *To Listen to a Child: Understanding the Normal Problems of Growing Up.* New York: Addison-Wesley, 1988.

Caine, Lynn. *What Did I Do Wrong? Mothers, Children, Guilt.* New York: Arbor House, 1986.

Canter, Lee, and Barbara Schadlow. *The Parent Conference Book.* New York: Canter & Associates, 1984.

Curran, Dolores. *Stress and the Healthy Family.* San Francisco: Harper & Row, 1985.

_____. *Traits of a Healthy Family.* San Francisco: Harper & Row, 1983.

Dinkmeyer, Don, et al. *The Effective Parent.* Circle Pines, MN: American Guidance Service, 1987.

Dinkmeyer, Don, and Jon Carlson. *Time for a Better Marriage.* Circle Pines, MN: American Guidance Service, 1984.

Dinkmeyer, Don, and Gary D. McKay. *Parenting Young Children: Helpful Strategies Based on Systematic Training for Effective Parenting—STEP—for Parents of Children Under Six.* Circle Pines, MN: American Guidance Service, 1989.

※_____. *The Parent's Guide: Systematic Training for Effective Parenting of Teens (STEP/Teen).* Circle Pines, MN: American Guidance Service, 1983.

_____. *The Parent's Handbook: Systematic Training for Effective Parenting (STEP).* Circle Pines, MN: American Guidance Service, 1982.

Doyle, Michael, and David Straus. *How to Make Meetings Work: The New Interaction Method.* New York: Jove Books, 1986.

Edmister, Patricia. "Establishing a Parent Education Resource Center." In *Changing Family Lifestyles: Their Effect on Children,* edited by James D. Quisenberry. Wheaton, MD: Association for Childhood Education International, 1982.

Einstein, Elizabeth, and Linda Albert. *Strengthening Your Stepfamily.* Circle Pines, MN: American Guidance Service, 1986.

Elmer, Elizabeth. *Growth and Development Through Parenting.* Chicago: National Committee for Prevention of Child Abuse, 1982.

Family Resource Coalition. *Family Resource Coalition Program Directory: A North American Network of Family Support Programs.* Chicago: Family Resource Coalition, 1982.

Furlong, J. Daryl. *A Ministry of Listening: Ministering with a Family Perspective.* Chicago: ACTA Publications, 1987.

Gesell, Arnold L., et al. *The Child from Five to Ten.* New York: Harper & Row, 1977.

Gordon, Thomas. *Leader Effectiveness Training.* New York: Bantam Books, 1984.

_____. *P.E.T. in Action.* New York: Bantam Books, 1978.

_____. *What Every Parent Should Know.* Chicago: National Committee for Prevention of Child Abuse, 1982.

Hagberg, Janet O. *Real Power: The Stages of Personal Power in Organizations.* San Francisco: Harper & Row, 1984.

Hayes, Cheryl D., and Sheila B. Kamerman, eds. *Children of Working Parents: Experiences and Outcomes.* Washington, DC: National Academy Press, 1983.

Kagan, Sharon L. *America's Family Support Programs: Perspectives and Prospects.* New Haven: Yale University Press, 1987.

Karpel, Mark A., ed. *Family Resources: The Hidden Partner in Family Therapy.* New York: Guilford Press, 1986.

Keniston, Kenneth, and the Carnegie Council on Children Staff. *All Our Children.* New York: Harcourt Brace Jovanovich, 1978.

Knowles, Malcolm S. *The Modern Practice of Adult Education: From Pedagogy to Andragogy.* New York: Cambridge Books, 1980.

Kolb, David. *Experiential Learning: Experience as the Source of Learning and Development.* Englewood Cliffs, NJ: Prentice-Hall, 1984.

L'Abate, Luciano, and Linda Young. *Casebook: Structured Enrichment Programs for Couples and Families.* New York: Brunner-Mazel, 1987.

Lawrence, Gerda, and Madeline Hunter. *Parent-Teacher Conferencing.* El Segundo, CA: TIP Publications, 1978.

Lerman, Saf. *Parent Awareness: Positive Parenting for the 1980's.* New York: Harper & Row, 1981.

_____. *Your Child from Six to Twelve.* New York: Harper & Row, 1985.

Lewis, Jerry M. *How's Your Family? A Guide to Identifying Your Family's Strengths and Weaknesses.* New York: Brunner-Mazel, 1989.

May, J. Gary. *Child Discipline: Guidelines for Parents.* Chicago: National Committee for Prevention of Child Abuse, 1982.

McLagan, Patricia A. *Helping Others Learn: Designing Programs for Adults.* Reading, MA: Addison-Wesley, 1978.

Mynatt, Elaine Simpson. *Remarriage Reality: What You Can Learn From It.* Knoxville: Elm Publications, 1984.

Napier, Rodney W., and Matti Gershenfeld. *Groups: Theory and Experience.* Boston: Houghton Mifflin, 1985.

Neville, Helen, and Mona Halaby. *No-Fault Parenting: A Practical Guide to Day-to-Day Life with Children Under Six.* New York: Facts on File, 1984.

Olson, David H., et al. *Family Inventories: Inventories Used in a National Survey of Families Across the Family Life Cycle.* St. Paul: University of Minnesota, 1982.

Pleck, Joseph H. *Working Wives/Working Husbands.* San Mateo, CA: Sage Publications, 1985.

Popkin, Michael. *Active Parenting: Teaching Cooperation, Courage, and Responsibility.* New York: Harper & Row, 1986.

Rogers, Fred, and Barry Head. *Mister Rogers Talks with Parents.* New York: Berkley Publishing Group, 1985.

Rothenberg, B. Annye, et al. *Parentmaking: A Practical Handbook for Teaching Parent Classes about Babies and Toddlers.* Menlo Park, CA: Banster Press, 1983.

Ryan, Patricia. *Single Parent Families.* Washington, DC: Supt. of Documents, Government Printing Office, 1981.

Samalin, Nancy, and Martha Moraghan Jablow. *Loving Your Child Is Not Enough: Positive Discipline That Works.* New York: Viking Penguin, 1988.

Schon, Donald. *The Reflective Practitioner: How Professionals Think in Action.* New York: Basic Books, 1984.

Shiff, Eileen, ed. *Experts Advise Parents: A Guide to Raising Loving, Responsible Children.* New York: Delacorte Press, 1987.

Smith, Robert M. *Learning How to Learn.* New York: Cambridge Books, 1982.

Smith, Robert M., ed. *Helping Adults Learn How to Learn.* San Francisco: Jossey-Bass, 1983.

Voydanoff, Patricia. *Work and Family Life.* San Mateo, CA: Sage Publications, 1987.

Yale Bush Center in Child Development and Social Policy, and The Family Resource Coalition. *Programs to Strengthen Families.* Chicago: Family Resource Coalition, 1983.

Groups, Organizations, Services

ACTA Publications, 4848 N. Clark St., Chicago, IL 60640-4711. (800) 825-0060.

Active Parenting, Inc., 810 Franklin Ct., Suite B, Marietta, GA 30067. (404) 429-0565.

American Association for Marriage and Family Therapy, 1717 K Street, NW, Suite 407, Washington, DC 20006. (202) 429-1825.

American Family Society, Box 800, Rockville, MD 20851. (301) 460-4455.

American Guidance Service, Publishers' Building, Circle Pines, MN 55014-1796. (800) 328-2560.

Association for Childhood Education International, 11141 Georgia Ave., Suite 200, Wheaton, MD 20902. (301) 942-2443.

Association for Children and Adults with Learning Disabilities, 4156 Library Rd., Pittsburgh, PA 15234. (412) 341-1515.

Center for the Improvement of Child Caring (CICC), 11331 Ventura Blvd., Suite 103, Studio City, CA 91604. (818) 980-0903.

Extension Service, Home Economics Program, U.S. Dept. of Agriculture, Washington, DC 20250. (Also contact the state or county agriculture extension services office or, at land-grant universities, the cooperative extension service.)

Families Anonymous, P.O. Box 528, Van Nuys, CA 91408. (818) 989-7841. (For concerned relatives and friends of youth with a wide variety of behavior problems.)

Families in the Nineties, 525 E. Mission Ave., Spokane, WA 99202. (509) 484-6733.

Family Development Resources, Inc., 219 E. Madison St., Eau Claire, WI 54703. (715) 833-0904.

Family Information Services, 12565 Jefferson St. NE, Suite 102, Minneapolis, MN 55434. (800) 852-8112; (612) 755-6233.

Family Resource Coalition, 230 N. Michigan Ave., Suite 1625, Chicago, IL 60601. (312) 726-4750.

Family Service America, 11700 W. Lake Park Dr., Milwaukee, WI 53224. (414) 359-2111.

Home and School Institute (HSI), Special Projects Office, 1201 16th St., NW, Washington, DC 20036. (202) 466-3633.

La Leche League, P.O. Box 1209, Franklin Park, IL 60131. (312) 455-7730.

Minnesota Curriculum Services Center, 3554 White Bear Ave., White Bear Lake, MN 55110. (612) 770-3943. (Offers numerous courses and guides, among them: *Families After Trauma, Fathering Curriculum, Guide for Developing Early Childhood Family Education, Self-Esteem and the Discouraged Child, Handling Anger Within the Family, Building Strong Families, Adults in Transition, The Middle Years, Experiencing Unemployment as a Couple, Changing Rural Lifestyles,* and *Parenting with a Global Perspective.*)

National Association for the Education of Young Children, 1834 Connecticut Ave., NW, Washington, DC 20009. (800) 424-2460.

National Committee for Prevention of Child Abuse, 332 S. Michigan Ave., Suite 950, Chicago, IL 60604. (312) 663-3520.

National Council on Family Relations (NCFR), 1910 W. County
Rd. B, Suite 147, St. Paul, MN 55113. (612) 663-6933.
(Includes the Family Resource Data Base—a computerized
library with wide-ranging references to parenting-related
courses, workshops, periodicals, and other documents—
offered through NCFR's Family Resource and Referral Center.)

National Organization of Adolescent Pregnancy and Parenting,
P.O. Box 2365, Reston, VA 22090. (703) 435-3948.

National PTA, 700 N. Rush St., Chicago, IL 60611. (312)
787-0977.

National Self-Help Clearinghouse, City University of New York,
33 W. 42nd St., New York, NY 10036. (212) 840-1259.

Parents Anonymous, 6733 S. Sepulveda Blvd., Suite 270, Los
Angeles, CA 90045. (800) 421-0353.

Search Institute, 122 W. Franklin, Suite 525, Minneapolis, MN
55404. (612) 870-9511.

Stepfamily Association of America, Inc., 602 E. Joppa Rd.,
Baltimore, MD 21204. (301) 823-7570.

Stepfamily Foundation, Inc., 333 West End Ave., New York, NY
10023. (212) 877-3244.

YMCA Program Resources, 6400 Shafer Ct., Rosemont, IL 60018.
(708) 823-2895.

Periodicals

*Active Parenting: The Newsletter of Video-Based Parenting Educa-
tion.* 810 Franklin Ct., Suite B, Marietta, GA 30067. (404)
429-0565.

*Bureau of National Affairs Special Report Series on Work and
Family.* Circulation Dept., P.O. Box 40947, Washington, DC
20077-4928.

*Effective Parenting: An AGS Newsletter for Sponsors of Parent
Training.* American Guidance Service, Publishers' Building,
Circle Pines, MN 55014-1796. (800) 328-2560.

✦ *Family Relations: Journal of Applied Family and Child Studies.*
National Council on Family Relations, 1910 W. County
Rd. B, Suite 147, St. Paul, MN 55113. (612) 633-6933.

The Family Therapy Networker. 7703 13th St., NW, Washington, DC 20012. (202) 829-2452.

Journal of Marital and Family Therapy. American Association for Marriage and Family Therapy, 1717 K St., NW, Suite 407, Washington, DC 20006. (202) 429-1825.

Marriage and Divorce Today: The Newsletter for Professionals Involved with Family, Couple, and Single Parent Issues. 2315 Broadway, New York, NY 10024.

Marriage and Family Living. Abbey Press, Hwy. 545, St. Meinrad, IN 47577. (812) 357-8011.

Newsletter of Parenting. Highlights for Children, 803 Church St., Honesdale, PA 18431. (717) 253-1080.

Parenting Studies. Eterna Press, P.O. Box 1344, Oak Brook, IL 60522. (312) 969-0318.

Public Affairs Pamphlets. New York Public Affairs Committee, 381 Park Ave. S., New York, NY 10016. (212) 683-4331.

Source Newsletter. Search Institute, 122 W. Franklin, Suite 525, Minneapolis, MN 55404. (612) 870-9511.

Stepfamily Bulletin: A Publication of the Stepfamily Association of America, Inc. 602 E. Joppa Rd., Baltimore, MD 21204. (301) 823-7570.

Stepfamily Foundation Newsletter: A Publication of the Stepfamily Foundation, Inc. 333 West End Ave., New York, NY 10023. (212) 877-3244.

Programs, Workbooks, Workshops

ACTA Publications. *Your Family of Origin* (tape series). 4848 N. Clark St., Chicago, IL 60640-4711.

Albert, Linda, and Elizabeth Einstein. *Strengthening Stepfamilies.* American Guidance Service, Publishers' Building, Circle Pines, MN 55014-1796.

Bonkowski, Sara. *Kids Are Nondivorceable: A Workbook for Divorced Parents and Their Children.* ACTA Publications, 4848 N. Clark St., Chicago, IL 60640-4711.

Canter, Lee, and Marlene Canter. *Assertive Discipline for Parents Workshop Kit*. Canter & Associates, Inc., P.O. Box 2113, Santa Monica, CA 90406.

Center for the Improvement of Child Caring. *Parenting Instructor Training Workshops*. 11331 Ventura Blvd., Suite 103, Studio City, CA 91604.

Dinkmeyer, Don, et al. *The Next STEP: Effective Parenting Through Problem Solving*. American Guidance Service, Publishers' Building, Circle Pines, MN 55014-1796.

_____. *PREP for Effective Family Living*. American Guidance Service, Publishers' Building, Circle Pines, MN 55014-1796.

Dinkmeyer, Don, and Jon Carlson. *TIME: Training in Marriage Enrichment*. American Guidance Service, Publishers' Building, Circle Pines, MN 55014-1796.

Dinkmeyer, Don, and Gary D. McKay. *Early Childhood STEP: Systematic Training for Effective Parenting of Children Under Six*. American Guidance Service, Publishers' Building, Circle Pines, MN 55014-1796.

_____. *STEP: Systematic Training for Effective Parenting*. American Guidance Service, Publishers' Building, Circle Pines, MN 55014-1796.

_____. *STEP/Teen: Systematic Training for Effective Parenting of Teens*. American Guidance Service, Publishers' Building, Circle Pines, MN 55014-1796.

Dunn & Hargitt, Inc. *Growing Up: The Parents' Newsletter Sent Home from School with the Student*. P.O. Box 620, Lafayette, IN 47902.

Evans, Marla D. *This Is Me and My Two Families: An Awareness Scrapbook/Journal for Children Living in Stepfamilies*. Brunner-Mazel, Inc., 19 Union Sq., New York, NY 10003.

Family Development Resources, Inc. *Developing Nurturing Skills for Parents and Children Workshops*. 219 E. Madison St., Eau Claire, WI 54703.

Fischhoff, Andi. *Birth to Three: A Self-Help Program for New Parents*. Castalia Publishing Co., P.O. Box 1587, Eugene OR 97440.

Gordon, Sol. *Sex: A Topic for Conversation—Three Video Programs.* Active Parenting, Inc., 810 Franklin Court, Suite B, Marietta, GA 30067.

Lerman, Saf. *Responsive Parenting.* American Guidance Service, Publishers' Building, Circle Pines, MN 55014-1796.

Loescher, Liz. *Conflict Management: A Curriculum for Peacemaking.* Conflict Center, 2564 S. Yates, Denver, CO. 80219.

National Governors' Association. *Focus on the First Sixty Months: A Handbook of Promising Prevention Programs for Children Zero to Five Years of Age.* 444 N. Capitol St., Washington, DC 20001.

Popkin, Michael H. *Active Parenting.* Active Parenting, Inc., 810 Franklin Court, Suite B, Marietta, GA 30067.

Pratt, Marion W. *The Positive Parenting Program.* Parent Learning Center, 4629 Bryce at Camp Bowie, Fort Worth, TX 76107.

Reivich, Joan S., and Yvonne L. Fraley. *The Parent Education Curriculum.* Family Support Center, Yeadon, PA 19050.

Samalin, Nancy. *Parent Guidance Workshops.* 180 Riverside Dr., New York, NY 10024.

Yehl, Suzy, and Medard Laz. *Rainbows for All Children: An Effective School Support Program for Children Who Live in Single-Parent Families, Step-Families, or Families in Painful Transition.* 913 Margret St., Des Plaines, IL 60016.

YMCA Program Resources. *Peoplemaking Thru Family Communication.* 6400 Shafer Ct., Rosemont, IL 60018.

Appendix A

Rewards and Strains in the Two-Career Marriage

Because husbands and wives often do not perceive the same issues as stressful, we suggest you choose from the following list the top five that have created the most stress in your family life. Number them in order of intensity, 1 being the most stressful. Then, if you choose to do so, guess which five are most stressful to your spouse. Exchange and discuss. Finally, take one step toward dealing with the number 1 stress named by each of you.

_____ daily child care

_____ sick child care

_____ fatigue

_____ lack of personal time

_____ lack of shared responsibility in the home

_____ differing housekeeping and yard standards

_____ latchkey child care

_____ insufficient money

_____ disagreement on spending

_____ paycheck issues: who pays for what

_____ too tired for sex

_____ lack of couple time

_____ lack of family fun time

_____ volunteerism: too little/ too much

_____ work vs. family time expectations

_____ intimacy needs unmet

_____ disagreement over whose job is more important

_____ shared parenting

_____ little time for spiritual growth

_____ depression: "Is this all there is?"

_____ disagreement over spouse's working

_____ children's sports and other activities

_____ work-related travel

_____ employer expectations/ demands

_____ children's school issues

_____ children's needs, fears, demands

_____ church/societal attitudes toward women working

_____ procrastination/deferring dreams

_____ perfectionism

_____ guilt over not getting
         everything done

_____ expectations and attitudes
         of your parents

_____ little time for friends

_____ other: _____

_____ other: _____

Specific steps we will take to reduce our top stresses:

1. _____

_____

_____

2. _____

_____

_____

Appendix B

Ages and Stages: A Closer Look*

1-year-old

- Is learning to walk, speak, explore (home should be baby-proofed)

2-year-old

- Is growing in motor, language abilities (almost daily leaps)
- Is trying to assert individuality
- May be negative, demanding
- Likes rituals
- Shows zest for life
- Is warm, affectionate

3-year-old

- Is more able to please, cooperate
- Has longer attention span
- Enjoys playing with friends
- May show temporary insecurity
- May seem uncoordinated at times; may stutter
- Daily routines can become source of conflict

4-year-old

- Is striving for new freedom, independence
- Behavior may be "out of bounds"—swearing, hitting, kicking
- Displays wide range of feelings
- Is sociable, lively, highly imaginative, eager to learn

9-year-old

- Shows greater independence, self-confidence
- Is busy with self-initiated projects, with friends
- Is pleasant companion to friends, family

10-year-old

- At climax point—feels especially good about self, world
- Enjoys, takes pride in family
- Likes position—not child, not teenager

11-year-old

- Is looking ahead to change; feels stress and turmoil
- Feels anxious about growing up
- Is starting to break away from parental influence; may challenge parent's views
- Is confused, argumentative; hard to live with at times
- Is prone to emotional outbursts
- May feel picked on
- Is increasingly capable as a person
- Maintains good peer relationships

12-year-old

- Is more peaceful, friendly, easygoing
- Feels pleased now to look toward growing up
- Demonstrates more mature behavior

5-year-old

- At interlude of harmony, time of contentment
- Is more mature—likely to use words rather than hitting
- Has strong motor skills
- Plays well alone, with others
- Is becoming more interested in reality rather than make-believe
- Is ready for some responsibility

6-year-old

- Is outgoing; is learning new skills
- Is self-centered
- Likes to be in charge, have own way; likes to win
- 6-year-old's mood shifts can be difficult for parents to take

7-year-old

- Is quiet; is assimilating growth, experience
- Is moody—may complain
- Shows increased interest in household responsibilities
- Shows increased consideration for others

8-year-old

- Feels self-confident; ready to tackle world
- Is cooperative, considerate
- Is making steady progress in skills, relationships

13-year-old

- Is introspective, searching for own identity
- Is touchy, sensitive to criticism
- Needs privacy

14-year-old

- Is more at ease with demands of adolescence, own growth
- Seems more personally content
- Has better, more satisfying personal relationships

15-year-old

- Feels anxious about soon joining adult world
- Feels pang to leave home; but yearns, strives for freedom, too
- Wants, needs to make independent decisions
- May be noncommunicative at home; spends good deal of time with friends

16-year-old

- Is more mature, self-appreciating
- Acts more responsibly, feels satisfied with gains in independence
- Feels on fairly equal footing with adults
- Is easier to get along with

*Information presented on this chart applies to boys and girls alike.

Appendix C

A Survey on Family Stress

Dear Parents:

Many of you have shared with us your frustration over a too-busy family calendar. Others of you have asked for help in establishing more quality family time together. We're interested in learning more about your specific needs so we may develop appropriate support for you and your families in these important areas. Your thoughts are important to us, and we invite you to share them with us by rating each item below as "Very Important," "Somewhat Important," or "Not At All Important" to your family.

I would like to know more about:

	Very Important	Somewhat Important	Not At All Important
Family Calendar			
Sharing child care in the two-paycheck family.			
Helping my child choose activities and schedule time wisely.			
Learning to weigh and organize family activities with an eye toward more time together.			
Looking at Little-League-type sports: their costs and benefits to family life.			
Dealing with special time stresses in the single-parent family.			
Other (specify): _____			
_____			
Television			
Learning more about the effects of television on healthy family life.			
Learning to use TV to bring the family closer together by discussing programs and the values in them.			
Sharing techniques for controlling the quality and quantity of TV in my home.			
Other (specify): _____			
_____			
Parent Needs			
Finding "me" time and space.			
Sharing ideas on men's and women's roles today: can I be both a good parent and a successful employee?			

	Very Important	Somewhat Important	Not At All Important

Dealing with self-image and guilt: failing to live up to my own expectations.

Other (specify): _____

_____

Volunteerism

Learning when and how to say no without feeling guilty.

Finding ways of volunteering, even with work and a family.

Finding ways to volunteer as a family.

Other (specify): _____

_____

Family Time Together

Dealing with stressful times and circumstances in the family: Christmas, vacation, the pre-dinner hour, illness, addiction, fighting, discipline (circle those of interest and add others): _____

Making our dinner hour a time of sharing and support.

Learning to communicate feelings as well as words: listening and responding.

Finding time to nurture family spirituality.

Learning how to have fun together as a family, with inexpensive recreation.

Other (specify): _____

_____

Additional Areas I Would Like Help On in Dealing with Family Stress: _____

_____

_____

_____

I have _____ children whose ages are _____. I (do/do not) work outside the home. The best day of the week for me to meet is _____, or _____; the best time is _____.

Please return via the enclosed stamped and addressed envelope. We will let you know the results of this survey. Thanks for sharing with us.

Appendix D

Family Strengths and Stresses

Listed below in order of priority are the fifteen traits chosen by 551 family participants as traits most commonly found in families they consider healthy. Prioritize these traits as you evaluate them in your own family, 1 being your strongest trait and 15 your weakest trait.

_____ 1. The healthy family communicates and listens.

_____ 2. The healthy family affirms and supports.

_____ 3. The healthy family teaches respect for others.

_____ 4. The healthy family develops a sense of trust.

_____ 5. The healthy family has a sense of play and humor.

_____ 6. The healthy family shares responsibility.

_____ 7. The healthy family teaches right and wrong.

_____ 8. The healthy family has a strong sense of kinship, with many traditions.

_____ 9. The healthy family has a balance of interaction.

_____ 10. The healthy family has a shared religious core.

_____ 11. The healthy family respects the privacy of its members.

_____ 12. The healthy family values service to others.

_____ 13. The healthy family fosters table time and conversation.

_____ 14. The healthy family shares leisure time.

_____ 15. The healthy family admits to problems and seeks help.

Listed below in order of priority are the ten stresses named most often by 660 families and parents surveyed.

To identify your family stresses and your spouse's perception of stresses, number these from 1 to 10, with 1 creating the most stress in your family life and 10 the least.

Compare your selection with that of your spouse.

_____   1. Economics/finances/budgeting

_____   2. Children's behavior/discipline/sibling fighting

_____   3. Insufficient couple time

_____   4. Lack of shared responsibility in the family

_____   5. Communicating with children

_____   6. Insufficient personal or "me" time

_____   7. Guilt for not accomplishing more

_____   8. Couple relationship (communication/friendship/sex)

_____   9. Insufficient family playtime

_____   10. Overscheduled family calendar

Appendix E

The Family Life Cycle

Stage One: *Courtship*

Rewards: _____

_____

Losses: _____

_____

Spiritual Tasks: _____

_____

Stage Two: *Birth of First Child*

Rewards: _____

_____

Losses: _____

_____

Spiritual Tasks: _____

_____

Stage Three: *Last Child Leaves for School*

Rewards: _____

_____

Losses: _____

_____

Spiritual Tasks: _____

_____

Stage Four: *Adolescence*

Rewards: _____

_____

Losses: _____

_____

Spiritual Tasks: _____

_____

Stage Five: *Disengagement or the Shifting Nest*

Rewards: _____

_____

Losses: _____

_____

Spiritual Tasks: _____

_____

Stage Six: *Empty Nest*

Rewards: _____

_____

Losses: _____

_____

Spiritual Tasks: _____

_____

Stage Seven: *Summation of Life*

Rewards: _____

_____

Losses: _____

_____

Spiritual Tasks: _____

_____

Appendix F

Five Methods of Dealing with Conflict

1. Avoidance _____

_____

_____

_____

2. Accommodation _____

_____

_____

_____

3. Competition _____

_____

_____

_____

4. Compromise _____

_____

_____

_____

5. Collaboration _____

_____

_____

_____

Appendix G

Sharing Responsibility in Our Family

1. Who in our family has the most responsibility for:

_____ Making money

_____ Saving money

_____ Household chores

_____ Settling fights

_____ Keeping the family mood up

_____ Pet care

_____ Driving members to activities

_____ Writing to grandparents

_____ Baby-sitting

_____ Reminding others of appointments

_____ Running errands

_____ Suggesting family fun

_____ Encouraging others in what they do

_____ Sympathizing when someone is blue

_____ Taking care of car and gas

_____ Yard care and snow removal

_____ Household repairs

_____ Monitoring heat, water, and
electricity use

_____ Other: _____

2. Compare responses. Where do we agree? Disagree?

_____

_____

_____

3. Who does too much? Who could do more?

_____

_____

_____

4. List three specific, achievable actions that could better balance our family responsibility right away. (Examples: agree that the house doesn't have to be so clean; take turns feeding the cat and cleaning the litter box; everybody settles fights, not just Mom.)

_____

_____

_____

_____

_____

_____

Appendix H

Taking Time to Look at Family Time

Time pressures lead to high stress in our lives, yet few of us take time to examine our use of time. Listed below are familiar uses of time in the family. At the end of the week, estimate the percentage of nonsleeping, nonworking time devoted to each area in your family. (Housework and cooking are considered work.) If, at the end of three weeks, you find consistent areas of imbalance, take at least one practical and immediate step to get your family time into balance.

The following is an example of time used in an imbalanced manner:

5% couple time
15% personal time
5% family playtime
60% children's activities
14% volunteerism
1% spiritual time

Activity	Week 1	Week 2	Week 3
Couple time (does not include watching TV together)	___	___	___
Personal time (TV, jogging, organizations)	___	___	___
Family playtime	___	___	___
Children's activities	___	___	___
Volunteerism	___	___	___
Visiting/caring for parents	___	___	___
Spiritual time	___	___	___
Other: _____	___	___	___